WHAT OTHERS ARE SAYING ABOUT CLINT:

". . . holding back tears from laughing so hard."
—*PopSugar*

"I think [Clint] is hilarious!" —*Kelly Clarkson*

"Edwards . . . reveals a very realistic perspective on parenting."
—*Reader's Digest*

PRAISE FOR *I'M SORRY . . . LOVE, YOUR HUSBAND*:

"Clint Edwards says he has no idea what he's doing, but I think he's a liar. *I'm Sorry . . . Love, Your Husband* is a wonderful combination of humor and heart!" —**Jen Mann,** *New York Times* bestselling author of *People I Want to Punch in the Throat*

"If anyone has ever asked you what it's like to be a parent, direct them to this book." —**Hollis Miller,** Huffington Post Parents

"Clint is a hands-on dad who just gets it. I was literally laughing out loud reading this." —**Jonna Miller,** the mother behind the viral sensation Real Blunt Blonde

PRAISE FOR *SILENCE IS A SCARY SOUND*:

"This book finally answers the age-old question of 'How many snakes do I take away from the toddler after he hits an elderly woman in the face with one?' (All but one, apparently)." —**Jenny Lawson,** *New York Times* bestselling author of *Furiously Happy*

"A funny and refreshing book that reminds us all that children are a perfect source of entertainment—as long as they belong to somebody else." —**James Breakwell,** author of *Bare Minimum Parenting* and *Only Dead on the Inside*

FATHER -ISH

LAUGH-OUT-LOUD TALES FROM A DAD TRYING NOT TO RUIN HIS KIDS' LIVES

CLINT EDWARDS

Author of *I'm Sorry . . . Love, Your Husband* and *Silence is a Scary Sound*

PAGE STREET
PUBLISHING CO.

PAGE STREET
PUBLISHING CO.

TO PIKACHU, THE FAMILY DOG:
The kids wanted to name you Fart Squirrel.
I objected.
You're welcome.

FATHERHOOD IS GREAT BECAUSE YOU CAN RUIN SOMEONE FROM SCRATCH.

—JON STEWART

SPECIAL OCCASION FAILS

CONTENTS

EVERYDAY FAILS

I KINDA SUCK
AT THIS . . .

In 2019, I was interviewed on an international TV show about how I manage screen-time limits with my children. They presented me as a parenting expert, something I find unsettling for a few reasons, the most pressing being that the title of my blog is No Idea What I'm Doing.

The interview was on Skype. I did it in my upstairs closet because it was the cleanest room in my house. But it was a big closet, and my hope was that they'd assume I had a home office, which I don't.

I JUST DIDN'T SEE THE POINT IN WEARING PANTS IF NO ONE WAS GOING TO SEE BELOW MY WAIST, SO I TUCKED MY SHIRT INTO MY UNDERWEAR AND REFUSED TO STAND UP FOR ANYTHING.

I was also in my underwear.

Okay, hold the phone: Perhaps that's misleading. I just didn't see the point in wearing pants if no one was going to see below my waist, so I tucked my shirt into my underwear and refused to stand up for anything.

(The real question is: Am I wearing pants right now as I type? Well, just don't ask me to stand up. Deal?)

To make matters worse, the TV show also left out the part where I mentioned that all of the good ideas I presented about managing screen time weren't mine at all.

They were my wife's.

What I'm trying to get at here is that although I was presented as a parenting expert for a few hot minutes on international TV, I wasn't.

I'm not.

I probably never will be.

I was just some dude trying to conceal all of his family's messes by hiding in his closet, which seems like an overarching metaphor for parenting in the twenty-first century, don't you think?

A few years ago, my wife, Mel, and I paid for pictures. The photographer took us to this very nice little bridge next to a stream in the Oregon woods. It was fall, and all three of our children left the van in adorable matching white and blue outfits, their hair combed just right.

The sun was setting. It was the magic hour.

We were there for who knows how long, fighting with our kids, giving them those bloodshot, silent, angry eyes that only parents get during family pictures, trying to get them to stop shoving dead leaves in their dress clothes.

I got so flustered, I had an emotional aneurysm.

Something broke in my head.

I think it was my sanity.

Or maybe my soul.

At one point I tried to put our toddler, Aspen, on my shoulders for a picture, and she kicked me in the face. Have you seen *Ant-Man*? When the hero shrinks down to the size of an ant, he can still punch with the power of a 200-pound (90.7-kg) man. I'm not sure of the science, but that kick to the face made me wonder if my daughter was actually Ant-Man.

AT ONE POINT I TRIED TO PUT OUR TODDLER, ASPEN, ON MY SHOULDERS FOR A PICTURE, AND SHE KICKED ME IN THE FACE.

My lip started bleeding and everything.

Out of the hundreds of pictures we took before the sun went down, we ended up with only one decent picture: a very adorable shot in which Aspen was looking up at her older sister Norah with admiration.

I posted it on my blog's Facebook page and it received hundreds of comments about how cute my kids were, and people complimented me on how good of a father I was.

I couldn't help but notice the irony as I read

through these comments with a bag of frozen peas on my lower lip.

I regularly get messages from people who follow me on social media, telling me I'm a great dad. They ask me for advice on their marriage and raising their kids as if I'm some sort of an expert. And every single time it happens, I look at the message and feel like a fraud. I don't know if this is impostor syndrome or what. I suppose it could be a lot of things, but one thing I know for sure is that I fail a lot as a father. Not that I don't have good ideas. I do. It's just that they often come out sideways.

THEY ASK ME FOR ADVICE ON THEIR MARRIAGE AND RAISING THEIR KIDS AS IF I'M SOME SORT OF AN EXPERT. AND EVERY SINGLE TIME IT HAPPENS, I LOOK AT THE MESSAGE AND FEEL LIKE A FRAUD.

I've written about parenting for the *New York Times* and the *Washington Post*. I've been presented as an expert on *The View* and *The Kelly Clarkson Show* and *The TODAY Show* and *Good Morning America*, and it's all a total sham because I sorta suck at this.

I started this parenting thing in 2007. Or was it 2006?

Wow . . . I feel like I'm at the doctor's office and they asked about my kids' birthdays.

It doesn't matter, because I've been at this for a while. I've done some really boneheaded things raising Tristan, Norah, and Aspen. I don't think any of them have been illegal—but definitely questionable and highly relatable.

FAILURE IS A HUGE PART OF BEING A PARENT.

I cannot be alone here. I think all parents have been living a normal life, doing their normal parenting thing, and *bam*! The sex talk happens. Or you think you've got it figured out, and suddenly you find your child's booger collection. Or you spend all day planning a wonderful birthday party and everything goes to hell, and somehow, as you are sitting there questioning your life choices, your child goes on and on about how awesome their party was and you are left wondering if maybe you are only half bad at this parenthood thing.

Failure is a huge part of being a parent. Sometimes you fail and learn a lesson. Sometimes fails are fails and nothing really good comes from them, but you try again tomorrow. Sometimes you feel like a failure, only to realize it was all in your head and you actually nailed it.

Failure is a natural part of parenting, and that is a fact that everyone online is trying desperately to hide.

Come on, now.

Admit it.

You didn't post about that time you lost it with your kids because they wouldn't get in the shower, or wouldn't let you sleep, or wouldn't stop asking for screen time, or kept arguing over whose fart smelled the worst, so you angry-whispered at them. But you really wanted to scream until you realized it was summer, and all the windows were open, and the neighbors would hear.

We are all like some dude in his closet doing a Skype interview on international TV, trying to look like an expert when in fact he's wearing a collared shirt and no pants.

There are no parenting experts.

I know this is a difficult notion to accept, considering everyone online presents themselves all put together with their quality pictures of smiling children with clean faces and well-organized rooms in the background. But that's all fake news, people. Behind each and every one of those pictures is a parent flipping their biscuits because their children won't stop shoving dead leaves in their pants.

So here's what I'm going to do in this book: I'm going to put myself out there. I'm going to tell a few stories where I didn't shine all that brightly as a father. I'm going to overreact and underreact. At times I will embellish and exaggerate, getting lost in my own fears or getting too excited when I should've been grounded—all of it causing me to say, think, or do something stupid. But please realize that in between these essays are a million moments where I shined so brightly as a dad it would have given you a farmer's tan.

Parenting is a huge gamble, and the possibility of 100 percent success is unlikely. Learn from my mistakes, and don't be surprised when you see a lot of yourself in these pages. And with that, I'm going to end this introduction with a truth: Failing but not giving up, day after day until your children begin to resemble functioning adults, really is the purest form of love.

SPECIAL OCCASION FAILS

WHEN SANTA
THREATENED
MY CHILDREN

I came into the kitchen late Saturday morning to find Tristan, my six-year-old son, on my cell phone. When I asked who he was talking to, he looked me dead in the eyes, holding the phone to his ear with his right hand, and said with fierce conviction, "Santa!"

It was midday, and his face was pale—a mix of shock and anger. I heard my old high school buddy John speaking on the other end of the line. He was grunting some. I didn't 100 percent know what had just happened until I took the phone from Tristan.

I spoke with John for a moment as Tristan watched. He was wearing black and yellow dump truck pajamas, his brown hair cut short on the scalp, blue eyes a mix of anger and confusion.

John told me he didn't realize it was Tristan on the phone, and he somehow managed to tell him everything about our Santa arrangement.

"I'm sorry, man. I blew it," he said.

It was days before Christmas. I'm not exactly sure how Tristan called Santa. I had a passcode on my smartphone. I remember reading a story a few years ago about the FBI not being able to get into a passcode-protected iPhone. Apple refused to help, and it all ended up in federal court. They could have saved everyone a lot of trouble by asking my six-year-old son for help. He was obviously a cell phone–hacking mastermind.

And to my son's credit, it was pretty ballsy of him to call Santa. I mean, seriously, what six-year-old calls Santa? I once sat on Santa's lap, looked in his twinkling eyes, and bawled. Then I peed my pants a little and my mother was all, "What is wrong with you? I thought you were a big boy!" And yeah, I was a big boy. But to a child, Santa is terrifying. He could decide on a whim he didn't like your smile and then cancel the entirety of your Christmas.

What a freaking power move.

IT WAS PRETTY BALLSY OF HIM TO CALL SANTA. I MEAN, SERIOUSLY, WHAT SIX-YEAR-OLD CALLS SANTA?

But I must say, Tristan calling Santa wasn't nearly as ballsy as what I'd been up to as his father most of that December.

Three weeks earlier, we were cleaning up the living room before going to pick up a Christmas tree when Tristan and his four-year-old sister, Norah, started fighting over who got to put away Bun-Bun, the stuffed bunny they both loved dearly. It was this stupid white Hallmark-store bunny with a blue hat and matching slippers and this half-smirking smile. Tristan found Bun-Bun at his grandmother's house a year earlier, and somehow it'd become our children's prized possession. They fought over who went to bed with it, who got to sit next to it at dinner, and who got to buckle it in the car before going places.

It was stained from being dragged along the ground, and the fur was nearly worn off on one side from being over-snuggled on alternating nights. Norah got to sleep with Bun-Bun on odd days of the week, while Tristan got the even days. My wife, Mel, and I actually had a schedule. It was like Tristan and Norah were divorced parents sharing custody of a child.

I hated Bun-Bun. I hated him more than I'd ever hated a real person, or animal, or anything really. Sometimes I lay awake at night and mentally broadcasted flickering films on the ceiling of Bun-Bun being tossed into a trash can fire. Before I became a father, I had no idea I could hate a stuffed bunny so much—but after being late to church each Sunday, all doctor appointments, and all parent-teacher conferences because I had to wait for my children to fight over who got to buckle a stuffed bunny into the car and then wait anxiously again as they repeatedly failed to buckle the bunny with their little uncoordinated fingers, I now understood that hating a stuffed bunny was a very real feeling. And yet I knew I couldn't actually toss Bun-Bun into a trash can fire because my children would be inconsolable. So I just put up with it, and somehow I think that made me the bunny's bitch.

Or my children's bitch.

It doesn't matter.

PEOPLE TALK A LOT ABOUT HOW PARENTING IS REWARDING, AND I WILL ADMIT THAT IT IS. BUT MOST OF IT'S ARGUING WITH YOUR CHILDREN.

Most of the year was like this. Me trying to get my children to pick up the living room, or get in the car, or keep their shoes on their feet, or go potty before we left the house, or stop fighting over who was going to sit next to Bun-Bun. They would undermine all my efforts by sneaking into another room to watch TV or by hiding in the bathroom to "poop" (an avoidance strategy I'd used a million times as a father and could see a mile away).

People talk a lot about how parenting is rewarding, and I will admit that it is. But most of it's arguing with your children to do something basic, only for them to dig in their heels as if picking up the living room was the hill they will die on.

The only exception is Christmastime.

It's the threat of Santa watching, knowing, and waiting for just one reason to withhold all Christmas gifts that made the holiday season something extra special for me as a father.

My children worked hardest at Christmastime, and after eleven months of arguing with Tristan and Norah over every little thing, the threat of Santa was as addictive as any drug. Is that the right metaphor? Maybe it was more of a power trip. I don't know exactly, but what I can say is that few things have been more rewarding in my life as a parent than being able to say, "Santa is watching," and seeing my children look up at me with complete irrational terror and then actually do what I asked them to do.

IT'S GOT TO BE THE BEST THING SINCE FRUIT SNACKS OR, AS I LIKE TO CALL THEM, "LITTLE BAGS OF SHUT THE HECK UP."

As a father who is constantly on the cusp of one more argument, it's got to be the best thing since fruit snacks or, as I like to call them, "little bags of shut the heck up."

I looked my children dead in the face and said, "If you don't get the living room clean in the next ten minutes, we will not have time to go get a tree, and if we don't get a tree, then Santa won't come because he won't have anywhere to put the gifts. Is that what you want?"

Tristan was gripping Bun-Bun by his head, while Norah was holding his legs. Both had angry, blue-eyed faces.

Tristan looked at me with one hand on his hip and the other still holding fast to Bun-Bun, his eyes half twisted, his lips in a confident smirk, and said, "Santa won't skip our house."

"Oh, really?" I said.

I pointed at the Elf on the Shelf®. He was sitting comfortably on our entertainment center in his little red pajamas, arms folded in his lap, leaning against a family picture and giving Tristan the side-eye.

"Thurchy is watching," I said.

It was a terrible name, even for an elf.

Tristan named him when he was four, which means we'd had that stupid, creepy, side-eying Orwellian nightmare watching our children and reporting to Santa for two years now. And I will admit, when we got that sucker, he was the most terrifying thing ever. I just had to point at that little guy, and my kids would pause like they were robbing a gas station and had suddenly realized there was a camera behind the register. But after a few years, the elf didn't really have the same kick it once had.

The real problem was that I kept forgetting to move the elf each night, which ultimately caused me to lie about why he hadn't moved (see page 49), and I was starting to think that our children didn't believe the elf was real . . . or that he was dead. I suppose both are technically true, but I couldn't let them know that. I needed the elf to provide my children with substantial fear so I could get the living room cleaned up in a timely fashion, preferably before I officially snapped and torched the house.

It was a simple equation: "The elf is watching" equals "Do what Dad asks."

Or so I thought.

Nothing with children is ever really simple, and the elf was all part of a much larger Christmas lie Mel and I had been building on for years.

Before the elf, we made videos with the Portable North Pole, a website that would create a pretty realistic and overall startling video of Santa himself lecturing my children. As I recall, the thing had a few different settings that basically were nice, needs improvement, and naughty. I, like many parents at the time, set it to naughty, just to make sure my bases were covered. I have no regrets. Santa even said their names, opened a book with their pictures in it, and showed them around the North Pole. Then he told them they were naughty and mentioned some specific behavior they need to work on: picking up around the house, not fighting over stuffed bunnies, trying new food without gagging, wiping their own butts . . . I could go on, but you get the idea.

This must have been 2011 or 2012, so these videos were some groundbreaking technology for the time. Were I a child, these videos would have made me not only listen to my parents but also eat healthy, exercise regularly, and never have premarital sex. And sure, it did work pretty well with my kids for the first year. But by the second year, they just didn't care anymore. They shrugged it off as if magical, cookie-eating half-elves from the North Pole sent them threatening messages all the time.

So we moved on to the elf, but now that wasn't working so well and I was starting to feel like I'd lost control. And you know what, the more I think about it, that's what this all came down to: control. And as I write that, it sounds pretty bad. But unless you've lived with young children, you have no idea how out of control parenting makes you feel.

I seemed to be on a perpetual search to up the "Santa is not someone to trifle with" ante each year. I doubt I'd ever have gone as far as to invite the Krampus over, the central European half-goat, half-demon that follows Santa around and eats bad children. But I was always looking for some way to make it just a little more real for my kids. I needed them to believe that I had a direct line to Santa, and if they didn't pick up the living room— or anything else I wanted them to do—PDQ, Santa was going to fly right on by our house and give that My Little Pony play castle and *Angry Birds* catapult to a child who didn't rip their stuffed bunny in half.

And you know what? Tristan was right. My kids would have to do way more than not clean up the living room for me to cancel Christmas. I loved it just as much as they did. Heck, I was the most-hated guy at work because I started listening to Christmas music on November 1. And sure, I could've put coal in my children's gift boxes and presents in mine, just to prove a point. But wow— that would have made me a pretty big jerk, as if all these Christmas lies weren't bad enough.

But as Tristan called my bluff about Santa flying by, I felt a little panicky. I needed something more. I looked at Tristan and Norah, who were both still holding Bun-Bun, and before I realized what I was saying, it came out: "Heck yes, Santa will skip this house. I'm going to send him a text right now!" I don't want to say that I yelled this at them, but it was definitely a stern exclamation, my finger pointing at the ground, my face a little red (something similar to Bernie Sanders's regular speaking tone).

Norah wore the sweetest pink shirt with kittens on it, her brown hair cut just above the shoulders. She looked at me through wide open eyes, her mouth slightly ajar, and said, "You know Santa's phone number?"

I paused for a moment, mostly because I hadn't thought this all the way through.

"Yup!" I said. "Santa and I send each other cat pictures!" I emphasized "cat pictures" so the kids would know I was serious.

I cocked my head to the side, giving them a what-do-you-think-of-them-apples look.

Bun-Bun hit the floor.

Norah, the younger and more impressionable one, started cleaning again, her face red and terrified.

Tristan, the older skeptic, approached me in his blue *Angry Birds* T-shirt and black soccer shorts. He put out his hand. "Let me see your phone."

He looked up at me, his small, stout shoulders stern. I didn't really know what to do, so I told him I needed to "poop" and ran to the bathroom.

I was in the bathroom for a while, calling friends and hoping that one of them would be willing to impersonate Santa.

"Keep cleaning," I said through the bathroom door. "When I'm done, we will send Santa a text."

At first I was worried that whoever actually picked up would judge me. Perhaps they'd say I was taking it too far. But once I finally got hold of my old friend from high school, John, all of that went away, because he couldn't stop laughing after I told him what I was up to.

"You're a genius!" he said. Then he asked if I'd do the same thing with his kids, and suddenly I felt good about what I was doing.

Maybe too good.

Sadly, if Santa were real, I'd have to assume that he'd skip my house for pulling a stunt like this. And I'd probably deserve it.

I changed John's name to "Santa" in my phone and even went as far as to upload a photo of Santa into his profile.

I stepped out of the bathroom and showed Tristan this text from Santa.

"How's the cleaning going?"

His mouth dropped.

"Wait," I said. On the phone was a string of dots.

"He's writing something else," I said.

Norah was looking at the phone now. Tristan was the only one who could read, so he read this message to her, his voice trembling ever so slightly. When I think back on this moment, he might as well have been getting a message from God. He was holding my hand as I held the phone. His palms were sweaty.

"I don't want to have to skip over your house this year. I hope the wee ones are being good! I have a lot of good things for your children. It would be very sad, but children have to be nice and do what their parents ask of them. I have to follow the rules. . . ."

It was the "follow the rules" part that really got them. Both kids seemed to have a lightbulb moment as they realized that there might just be an outside set of rules that Santa had to follow.

Rules that were not subject to leniency.

To say the next few weeks were glorious was an understatement. All I had to do was reach into my pocket for my phone and my children would get busy. It didn't really matter what it was: pick up the living room, clean off the table, use the potty before leaving, get in the van, stop fighting. At one point, I even had Tristan cleaning the toilets. With Santa in my pocket, any job I didn't want to do was delegated to my children.

No fuss, no muss.

And just to keep it alive, Santa sent periodic threats. Well, maybe they weren't threats in the "I'm going to murder you" Hollywood movie kind of way. They were nice threats, you know . . . from Santa.

"I heard Tristan splashed a bunch of water out of the tub yesterday and didn't clean it up. That's too bad. I'd just asked one of my elves to build him an iPad. But now I'm going to have to cancel that order."

AND JUST TO KEEP IT ALIVE, SANTA SENT PERIODIC THREATS.

The crazy thing is, I never once felt like I was doing anything wrong until my wife started asking questions. Listen, when I think back on this moment now, I can't help but admit that what I was doing probably warped my children in some long-term way that will manifest the moment they become a YouTube sensation. And subconsciously, I probably knew that, and it very well could have been the reason I didn't tell Mel about this whole Santa-texting thing. Not that I exactly hid it from her. I just didn't tell her. Or text Santa when she was around. I tried pretty hard to keep my children from saying anything about it. But when I read what I just wrote, it sure does sound like I was hiding it from her.

Okay, fine. So I hid this from my wife.

Happy?

Naturally, she did find out (like she always does), because I'm not all that good at hiding things. She started asking questions about why the children were being so well behaved. She couldn't understand why they would suddenly get to work each time I reached in my pocket. Eventually, I told her what I was up to.

OKAY, FINE. SO I HID THIS FROM MY WIFE. HAPPY? NATURALLY, SHE DID FIND OUT.

She didn't exactly say I was a sack of holiday garbage. She didn't say I sucked or that I was messing up the kids. She did something much, much worse: She gave me the "you need to grow up" look. It was the same look she often gave me when I did things like tell the kids we needed to amputate their leg because they scuffed their knee.

Then she told me I had to stop.

Actually, she told me I needed to admit what I was doing to the kids, but after some discussion on the matter, she admitted that wasn't the best idea because it might cause the children not to believe in Santa anymore. And no one wanted that. Seeing our children light up on Christmas morning and say those simple words—"Santa came!"—was not something either of us wanted to lose anytime soon.

"This is just too far," she said.

We went back and forth for a bit, and I at last reluctantly agreed to tell our children that Santa got a new phone and forgot to send me his new number. This was an altogether new lie that was going to make my original lie right—frankly, so much of my parenting at Christmastime had come down to this exact same line of reasoning. But I must admit, I wasn't really on board with the idea, so I dragged my feet for a few days. And it wasn't until Saturday morning, two days before Christmas, when Mel said she was going to tell them about Santa's new phone, that I finally went into the kitchen, ready to spill the spice drops, only to find Tristan on the phone with Santa.

I hung up the phone after John (a.k.a. Santa) told me he "blew it" and looked at my son.

His eyes were misty.

I was in this situation where I needed to come clean, but I wasn't sure exactly how clean to come.

I wanted him to continue believing in Santa. This is going to sound cliché, but as I looked at my son waiting for an explanation, I realized I'd forgotten what Christmas was all about. It wasn't about getting my children to do what I wanted them to do. It was about magic and love and giving.

He gave me this look that said, "You have some explaining to do."

I didn't know where to start.

I crouched down next to Tristan and said, "That wasn't Santa."

Tristan looked up at me with a flat expression that seemed to say, "Well, duh."

"It was my friend John. I don't have Santa's phone number. I never have. And I'm sorry for trying to make you believe that I did."

He looked at the ground, his left foot tapping our kitchen linoleum. He didn't call me a bad dad. He didn't run to his room and cry. All he said was, "Why?"

I took a breath. "I guess I just wanted you to listen to me. And since you didn't, I decided to try getting someone you might listen to. So I had my friend pretend to be Santa."

"So you don't know Santa?" Tristan asked.

I shook my head. "I'm not cool enough to know Santa. And I'm sorry that I lied."

Tristan's eyes moved side to side as he processed his own father admitting to a lie. Then he said in a very adult tone, "Well, I guess you are going to have to write him a letter and say you're sorry."

I laughed a little. Then I smiled down at him and said, "Do you think he'll forgive me?"

He shrugged and said, "Probably. Santa's a pretty nice guy."

"But do you forgive me?" I asked.

He thought about it for a moment and then replied, "If Santa forgives you, I'll forgive you."

I laughed again and said, "Well, I guess we better write that letter then."

MY CHILDREN WILL PROBABLY CHAT WITH A THERAPIST ABOUT THAT TIME WE BUILT A GINGERBREAD HOUSE

I must have sat in on a million training sessions on how to give a human the Heimlich maneuver, but never once had I been trained on how to do it for a dog. I didn't really have time to look up an instructional video on YouTube. The dog obviously wasn't breathing properly. He wheezed and coughed, his abdomen sunk well into his small body. His little brown eyes were watering as he fought for air.

I swept the little guy into my arms, hugged him to my chest as if he weren't actually a dog at all but just a small, furry, four-legged human, and started rubbing his underbody, searching for his belly button. Only it turns out he didn't have a belly button. Well, he might have had one. I don't know if dogs come with belly buttons. In the heat of the moment, I couldn't feel it. Not that he had a lot of belly to search. He was a small mutt of a thing, a rescue dog we picked up at the pound a few years earlier, with short brown fur and eyes and Baby Yoda ears. The kids named him Pikachu, and he looked like a mix of dachshund and Chihuahua. But to me, he looked more like a large rodent—an opossum, or maybe a nutria. Definitely not a Pokémon. Not that my opinion mattered when it came to pets. Everyone thought he was adorable: the kids, Mel, the mailman, the neighbors . . . everyone but me.

THE KIDS NAMED HIM PIKACHU, AND HE LOOKED LIKE A MIX OF DACHSHUND AND CHIHUAHUA. BUT TO ME, HE LOOKED MORE LIKE A LARGE RODENT.

Were it up to me, we wouldn't have a dog or a cat or anything with fur on it, but as a father of three, I didn't get to make those sorts of decisions because when it came to pets, it was all very democratic. And as a father who never wanted a dog but got one for no other reason than to benefit his children, I can say with certainty that the purest show of love I ever demonstrated to an animal was caring for Pikachu.

A few seconds? A minute? Two minutes? I don't know how long I spent searching for the right place to pump his little dog body to get the gingerbread out. I rubbed my hand up and down him as the family watched. I kept accidentally touching his little dog penis, and I must say, were I choking on gingerbread and someone kept touching my penis, I would probably be strangely aroused but on the whole, confused and frustrated. And I think I could feel all those emotions coming from our small family dog.

I eventually picked a spot somewhere below Pikachu's rib cage, hugged tightly, his back to my chest, and started pumping his body.

I KEPT ACCIDENTALLY TOUCHING HIS LITTLE DOG PENIS, AND I MUST SAY, WERE I CHOKING ON GINGERBREAD AND SOMEONE KEPT TOUCHING MY PENIS, I WOULD PROBABLY BE STRANGELY AROUSED BUT ON THE WHOLE, CONFUSED AND FRUSTRATED.

It was Christmas Eve. The Mariah Carey Christmas album played in the background of our small, rural Oregon home. The stockings were hung and our tree was up and glowing. It was dark outside, just after seven o'clock at night. The house smelled of pine, gingerbread, and ham, and I could see the lights of our neighborhood twinkling out the window. The scene was exactly how I'd always imagined Christmas as a father. Well, outside of my giving the dog the Heimlich maneuver.

In the middle of all this Christmas chaos, I was weighted with the underlying truth that if our family dog choked to death on Christmas Eve, it would surely be a tragedy, yes. But I also knew without a shadow of a doubt that I would be blamed.

I knew this in the core of my being.

THE SCENE WAS EXACTLY HOW I'D ALWAYS IMAGINED CHRISTMAS AS A FATHER. WELL, OUTSIDE OF MY GIVING THE DOG THE HEIMLICH MANEUVER.

The plan for that day was to build this epic gingerbread house with real homemade gingerbread and icing, along with some serious candy trimmings: spice drops, red hots, M&M's, gumballs, the works. We spent most of Christmas Eve baking gingerbread. We cut out a custom plan so it would be in the shape of our own house, and we made a little gingerbread family to place inside, including a gingerbread Pikachu. All of it was wholesome and adorable until the dog started dying.

We all circled the dinner table. Tristan was ten, Norah was eight, and little Aspen was already down for the night. The gingerbread was thick and heavy. I don't know if we baked it wrong or what, but the center was kind of spongy while the edges were hard as a rock. Think of the tater tots you got from the school cafeteria when you were a child: The centers were frozen and the outsides were a little burned. Our gingerbread was kind of like that.

I assumed the hard outer gingerbread would support the soft interior, but apparently I was wrong—by the time we built the thing, and added all the trimmings, and stood back and looked at it with awe, it collapsed.

THINK OF THE TATER TOTS YOU GOT FROM THE SCHOOL CAFETERIA WHEN YOU WERE A CHILD: THE CENTERS WERE FROZEN AND THE OUTSIDES WERE A LITTLE BURNED. OUR GINGERBREAD WAS KIND OF LIKE THAT.

It was a pretty epic crumble, I will admit. It started slowly, sliding off its foundation all tired and left-leaning, and suddenly crashing down in a blur of gingerbread and spice drops, crushing the gingerbread family we placed inside.

Tristan thought it was cool, Norah seemed emotional, and the dog, well . . . he just stuck his head under the table, begging for someone to drop something sweet or to take pity and give him a spice drop.

Listen, I will be 100 percent transparent here and say I wasn't mean to the dog. I was actually very good to him. I took him on walks and picked up his poop in the backyard. I gave him regular baths and I even subscribed to this once-a-month BarkBox thing that sent him new chew toys and exotic snacks like cow knees and dried pheasant. He met with a vet more times each year than I met with a doctor. He had a very nice raincoat and a Halloween costume, and let me tell you, he did make a very snuggly hot dog each October 31st. I was a good dog owner. Not to overstate our relationship, but I think he thought I was his best friend. At least all indications pointed in that direction. He got emotional when I left, and when I came home he greeted me at the door as though I were a returning champion, getting so excited that he peed a little. On the whole, it was flattering. No one else in my family peed a little when I got home. But at the same time, he peed a little every time I got home, and that just isn't awesome at all.

But that was life with our dog—everything was a double-edged sword, and it was commonly known that I didn't like the dog. I don't want to say that I hated Pikachu. I would never outwardly admit to that. My feelings for him were somewhere above hate but below love in this strange gray area, somewhere between animosity and annoyance, similar to how most people feel about the band Nickelback.

And you know what, I had some grievances that were valid. Mostly about typical irritating dog behavior.

HE MADE PASSIONATE LOVE TO OUR FURNITURE, SOMETHING I NEVER UNDERSTOOD, CONSIDERING HE'D BEEN NEUTERED; BUT NEVERTHELESS, I SEEMED TO BE REGULARLY SCRUBBING HIS "LOVE STAINS" OFF OUR COUCH PILLOWS.

He barked so much in the backyard our neighbors called the cops, he liked to sneak into the laundry room every time our kids left the door open and chew on our dirty clothing, and he was more or less an escape artist, sprinting into the neighborhood every time someone opened the front door. He made passionate love to our furniture, something I never understood, considering he'd been neutered; but nevertheless, I seemed to be regularly scrubbing his "love stains" off our couch pillows. According to our vet this was some sort of a phase.

I complained about Pikachu constantly. When he ran away, I was always a little casual about it, saying things like, "He'll come back." And then the children dragged me outside to go find him. Sometimes I daydreamed about his funeral in the backyard, a moment that felt very far in the future, considering I had looked up how long he might live and Google said 12 to 15 years, setting him up to live through several presidential administrations.

And there was no doubt that the children loved Pikachu unconditionally, and at times, I knew they loved him more than they loved me. Just a couple of days before this gingerbread incident, Norah swaddled the dog in a blanket and then cradled him in her arms like a baby. I'd just gotten home from work, so I went to give Norah a kiss on the forehead and ask about her day. She raised her hand, swatted me away, and told me to leave her alone.

"I only love Pikachu," she said.

Then she tipped her head down and Pikachu licked the inside of her mouth. He gave me this condescending look, like he was some low-life boyfriend I didn't approve of but who knew that if I voiced my disapproval I'd only be solidifying their relationship.

But now, as I am discussing this complicated relationship I have with our family dog, it might be a good time to admit that I wrote some of this book in our living room with Pikachu curled around my feet. And in those moments, it's hard not to feel like having him around is pretty okay.

And I know, it seems like I am circling around the real question: Was I trying to kill the dog with gingerbread? You know, I'll admit that the optics weren't good. I'm not going to try and compare our dog choking on gingerbread to the whole Jeffrey Epstein suicide debacle, but what I will say is that

I gave Pikachu the small gingerbread version of himself innocently.

AND I KNOW, IT SEEMS LIKE I AM CIRCLING AROUND THE REAL QUESTION: WAS I TRYING TO KILL THE DOG WITH GINGERBREAD? YOU KNOW, I'LL ADMIT THAT THE OPTICS WEREN'T GOOD.

I will also admit that the moment I gave him the gingerbread, Mel said, "Don't feed him that. He'll choke."

And I kid you not, I looked her right in the face and said, "It's Christmas Eve. Dogs don't choke on Christmas Eve."

But come on!

I had no idea that this would happen. He ate whatever my children dropped on the kitchen floor without choking. And to his credit, I will say that since we'd had him, our floor had never been cleaner.

I never fed the dog table scraps. According to the vet, Pikachu had a bit of a weight problem, so we had to buy him special weight-loss dog food and portion out his meals, a service many celebrities pay serious money for. But it was Christmastime and I had a little weight problem too, so I thought it might be nice to bury the hatchet, and love my neighbor, and give generously even to those that irritate you. So I gave him some gingerbread as a little treat, but it totally backfired. Now, as I write this essay about one of my biggest fatherly failures, I feel like I'm fighting to explain my actions in my own book, so that everyone reading won't think I tried to kill our family dog.

Furthermore, I am sure many of you reading this are wondering if I'd have given Pikachu the Heimlich maneuver if my wife and children weren't watching. And that's a valid question. Yes, I'd have tried to save his life regardless. But I will also add this clarifying statement: My primary motivation in those chaotic few moments was to save my own reputation. I didn't want to be blamed for murdering the dog on Christmas Eve. And when I think about that, it does seem pretty selfish. I have a feeling there are dog lovers reading this who are wishing that I were the one who choked.

I can understand that.

But let me say this: Unless you've cleaned stains off your couch pillows in the shape of little red rocket ships, please contain your judgment.

I tugged at his little body in jerking motions. I didn't know if I was doing it right, but I was giving it my best. It all came up violently, in a stew of dog food and gingerbread and stomach acid. It shot farther than I expected, and because I was standing, the pitch was just right, so it landed in a nasty glob on the collapsed gingerbread house, which seemed like a symbol, or metaphor, or something.

Regardless of what it all meant, the gingerbread house had collapsed, and it was now covered in dog puke, and the only family member who ate any of it was Pikachu, the member of our family I enjoyed the least. And that alone made this whole night before Christmas a huge fail.

But on the bright side, although my motivation for saving the dog's life might not have been pure, the kids hugged the dog. Then they hugged me and acted like I was a hero for saving his life, and it almost felt like I'd lit my own house on fire, put it out, and received a medal for heroism.

As I cleaned up the mess on our kitchen table and Mel worked on getting the kids to bed at a decent hour so we could place the presents under the tree, it was just Pikachu and I in the kitchen.

We made eye contact.

And I kid you not, I had the audacity to say, "You're welcome."

LIES I'VE TOLD
MY CHILDREN ABOUT
ELF ON THE SHELF

It all started out as a wholesome, festive way to get the kids to behave. But then something changed, and the Elf on the Shelf became a chore of moving the stupid thing and thinking on my feet. I'm kinda surprised our elf never went directly to the police over my lies.

Here are a few examples:

When you do something naughty, it causes the elf physical pain.

Family meeting! If you will all notice, the elf is on the towel rack today for two reasons. First, make sure you flush. Second, someone keeps blowing their nose on the towels. Rest assured, Santa will be getting to the bottom of this!

Kid: Why didn't he move?

Me: His legs are broken.

Kid: How did that happen?

Me: Someone must've touched him. *(Stares at kid for several seconds.)*

Kid: *(Looks at ground.)*

Kid: Who ate all of the chocolates from my advent calendar?

Me: *(Points at elf.)*

I didn't throw away your drawing. The elf took it as a gift for Santa—along with your recorder and that nasty farting dog puppet your grandma sent you.

He's still in the tree because he fell asleep waiting for you to fall asleep. You need to stop making the elf work overtime.

Wife: Who farted?

Me: *(Points to elf.)*

Sometimes he doesn't move because you don't believe enough. Tell the elf you're sorry.

Me: Santa punishes the elf when you do naughty things. If it gets bad enough, he sends a new elf.

Kid: What happens to the bad elves?
Me: You know the cream in Cadbury eggs?
Kid: Yeah.
Me: That's what happens to bad elves.

The elf doesn't blink because he doesn't
trust you.

Kid: Who does the elf love most?
Me: He loves you all equally.
Kid: Oh! Kind of like you.
Me: Yeah . . . exactly.

Wife: Who ate the last brownie?
Me: (*Points to elf.*)

Note pinned to backyard fence:
Please stop leaving the gate open. Every
time the dog gets out, I can't get back to
the North Pole. He's my ride.
—Thurchy the Elf

Yeah, well, it's complicated. The elf is a
little late this year because he joined a
union and now he only works 20 days
instead of 25.

Me: Did you wash your hands?
Kid: Yes.
Me: (*Glances at elf.*)

Kid: (*Walks back into the restroom.*)

Listen, kiddo. I don't see why I owe the
elf an apology letter. He was falling onto
the stove. I didn't want him to catch fire.
I saved his life! Okay. Fine. (Writes letter
to elf: "*I am sorry for saving your life.
Next time I'll let you burn. As Santa is my
witness, I will let . . . you . . . burn.*")

Kid: You're the best dad ever!
Me: Aw, thanks!
Kid (*whispering*): Do you think the elf
heard me?
Me: No. You better say it again.

THE TIME
MY SON REALIZED
I WAS SANTA

Our bishop reluctantly asked me to play Santa over the phone about two hours before the church Christmas party. He told me that the older, fatter, bearded man he'd originally asked was having some health problems and couldn't make it. "You expressed interest in doing this, and unless someone older and fatter walks in, I'm going to have to give you the job."

I didn't know how to take what he said. It seemed like he'd placed me in a lineup of potential Santas and said, "Well, he isn't all that fat, and he isn't all that old, and he isn't all that jolly, but he's what we've got." I probably would have felt more pride in the position if there had been stiffer competition. Perhaps a string of auditions, for example. Or maybe a Santa cage match. But instead it was one of those "You're the only option, which makes you the best option" sort of situations, which isn't a great boost for anyone's confidence.

He was right, though. I had expressed interest in the role. I'd kind of pestered him about it, actually, showing him my "Ho, ho, ho!" several times, as if the hallways of our church were any place for a Santa audition.

As he offered me the Santa gig, he reminded me that Norah and Tristan were five and seven.

"Are you sure you want to do this?" he said.

At the time, I wasn't sure what he was getting at. Looking back, I realize he was an older father with much older children who didn't believe in Christmas magic anymore. I think he was trying to warn me that I was risking my children losing their belief in Santa.

But I didn't think about that at all, because I was so freaking excited. This whole situation felt like a heartwarming 1950s TV show, where Dad dresses up like Santa and fools all the kids, and then they look back as adults and realize how much their father loved them and how good he was with disguises.

It felt like a Norman Rockwell painting.

This was going to be *the* defining moment of my fatherhood.

Tristan and Norah were going to sit on my lap, and I was going to tell them specifics about their lives, their behavior, their friends and family like I was some omnipotent god.

To say that I was feeling a misplaced rush of power was an understatement. . . .

In the church's main office, I transformed into Santa. It was a small room with a window in the door and an outdated personal computer. I put on an angel-hair beard with a matching wig. I stuffed the suit with a couple of decorative pillows I found in the foyer and practiced my "Ho, ho, ho!"

The Christmas party was being held in the basketball court of our Mormon church.

I'M SHORT—ABOUT 5 FEET, 7 INCHES— AND 170 POUNDS. I WASN'T BUILT TO PLAY BALL, AND INDEED, THE BISHOP WAS RIGHT: I WASN'T BUILT TO BE SANTA EITHER.

I recently found out that people assume all Mormons are awesome at basketball because most of our churches have a basketball court. Outside of a few party-hard years in my late teens and early twenties, I have been Mormon all my life, and I have the hand-eye coordination of a stumpy *Tyrannosaurus rex*. I'm short—about 5 feet, 7 inches—and 170 pounds. I wasn't built to play ball, and indeed, the bishop was right: I wasn't built to be Santa either.

At least not in the classic, Coca-Cola Santa way: a fat jolly man with a beard and wrinkles. I was in my early thirties at the time, and I wondered if my children would accept a younger and leaner Santa, or if they would look at my slender waistline and smooth eyes and tell me that I was full of fudge. Suddenly I felt a lot of pressure to perform, and the person I most worried about fooling was Tristan.

He was in a transitional age when it came to Santa. He wanted to believe, but his own curiosity for the adult world was getting the best of him. One year earlier, he'd called Santa on my cell phone (page 22), and although it seemed like he still believed, I had my doubts. As I stepped out of the office and into the basketball court, I had a feeling that this moment would either reinforce his belief in Santa or completely destroy it, so I really threw myself into the role.

I spoke in a husky, Santa-like baritone that burned my throat. I vigorously shook the bells sewn to the Santa coat hem. I'm not going to say I deserved an Oscar, but I at least matched the year Ernest P. Worrell saved Christmas.

I SPOKE IN A HUSKY, SANTA-LIKE BARITONE THAT BURNED MY THROAT. I VIGOROUSLY SHOOK THE BELLS SEWN TO THE SANTA COAT HEM. I'M NOT GOING TO SAY I DESERVED AN OSCAR, BUT I AT LEAST MATCHED THE YEAR ERNEST P. WORRELL SAVED CHRISTMAS.

Short, boogery-faced children rushed me, their arms out, hands slick with drool and cookie frosting, their eyes glossy, and their faces longing for affirmation that Santa had indeed noticed that they'd been good all year and would bring them that special something.

I looked down at the children as they tugged at my red velvet pants, which were supported with white candy cane–print suspenders, and chanted, "Santa! Santa!" I patted their heads like some kind of faith healer, blessing them with goodwill to men and repeated my slogan over and over: "Ho, ho, ho! Merry Christmas!"

I had a difficult time walking for a few reasons. One was the crowd of children, naturally. But there were also the paper-thin black plastic boots that came with the suit. They fit like grocery sacks and slid on the gym floor and kept falling down like a worn-out pair of socks.

This was obviously some discount knockoff outfit that didn't fit me very well. It most likely predated the Internet, but if it were ordered today, it probably would've come from wish.com. I kept waiting for one of the children to tug off my pants, exposing my fruitcake to the congregation. I could hardly see through the beard and wig. The suit was hot and itchy, and I was surprised by how quickly I went from jolly to grumpy.

Eventually I just started pushing children out of the way.

Near the back of the basketball court was a stage, and on the stage was a big red easy chair with a red Santa bag of candy beside it. I sat down.

To my left, children were already lining up, their legs jiggling, their eyes full of wonder.

The first to sit on Santa's lap was a little blonde girl I'd never seen before. I asked her name, and she looked at me like I was an approaching train. No response. I asked what she wanted for Christmas. Nothing. I asked if she'd been good all year, and she started crying. She looked at me as if I could peer into her soul, so I just handed her a bag of candy canes. She ran.

I ASKED IF SHE'D BEEN GOOD ALL YEAR, AND SHE STARTED CRYING. SHE LOOKED AT ME AS IF I COULD PEER INTO HER SOUL, SO I JUST HANDED HER A BAG OF CANDY CANES. SHE RAN.

The next was my five-year-old daughter, Norah. I got nervous as she crawled onto my lap. She looked up at me with wonder. She didn't recognize me at all. I thought about the power I had to influence her while I was playing Santa. I wondered what I might tell her that would make her a better person, perhaps motivate her to go to college or marry a charming and intelligent person rather than some lowlife with nice abs. But then I remembered that she was five and what I really wanted was for her to flush the toilet after a number two.

"What's your name, little girl?" I said a few octaves lower than usual. I coughed halfway through the question and my eyes got a little watery, all of it feeling very Christian Bale as Batman.

She looked me in the eyes, gave a sly half-grin, and said, "Norah."

I asked if she'd been good all year, and she vigorously nodded. Then I said, "You know, I was speaking with your elf, Thurchy. He said you haven't been flushing the toilet. Is this true, Norah?"

Norah looked at the stage floor.

"Hmmm . . ." I replied. "I've got that Snow Queen Elsa dress you asked for. It lights up and sings 'Let It Go.' But I don't know if you're ready for it just yet. I'm going to follow up with Thurchy before Christmas to see if you've been flushing the toilet." I raised my eyebrows and added, "I don't want to have to give it to Martha."

Norah glared at me.

Martha was a little brunette girl from church. They were best friends—supposedly—but we all knew they were frenemies.

A CHILD FAR TOO OLD TO BE SITTING ON SANTA'S LAP TOLD ME HE KNEW WHO I *"REALLY WAS."* I TOLD HIM THAT I REALLY WAS SANTA AND THAT I KNEW HOW TO BREAK INTO HIS HOUSE.

Norah nodded. I handed her a bag of candy, called her a good little girl, and gave her a hug.

That moment couldn't have gone any better.

I went through a few more children. Many of them looked at me with terror, some with awe, some with curiosity, others with suspicion. A child far too old to be sitting on Santa's lap told me he knew who I "*really was*." I told him that I really was Santa and that I knew how to break into his house.

It was the eye contact that got my point across.

Around this time, Mel walked past.

"Hey, pretty lady, have you been nice . . . or *naughty*?" I asked. Then I asked if she'd like to "hop up on Santa's lap." I patted my knee and winked.

She told me to grow up, and suddenly I felt like a naughty Santa.

It was a good feeling, but this may have been the creepiest thing I'd ever done.

Near the end of the party, Tristan crawled onto my lap, his face soft and somber, like he knew who was really behind the beard. Tristan's red Chuck Taylor All Stars dangled well above the floor while he sat on my lap. He was in a green hooded long-sleeve shirt and brown shorts.

When Tristan was four, I asked him how much candy I'd have to give him to stay four forever. He answered, "Ten, ten, ten, and seven."

I gave him a handful of chocolate chips from the pantry. Then we shook hands. At the time, I was serious. I loved him at that age. I wanted him to be sweet and cute and little forever. I sometimes told my kids that their crap would be on the curb once they turned eighteen, but in actuality, I didn't want them to grow up and move on.

I wanted them to stay young and innocent forever.

But as Tristan sat on my lap, I swore I could see the innocence of his youth draining away, and I wondered if dressing up as Santa had forced him to grow up a little faster—and that fact made me feel a pit in my gut.

I asked his name.

"Tristan," he said.

Then we went through the motions, my asking if he'd been a good boy and his saying yes. He told me what he wanted, I gave him a bag of candy. He got off my lap and as he walked away, he turned to give me one last knowing look.

I sat in the chair a little longer, chatting with different children. Tristan lingered next to the stage. After the last child had visited with Santa, I headed back to the church office. Halfway across the basketball court, I turned around and noticed a gang of children following me. I can't give you exact numbers here, but it didn't matter. When you're in a Santa suit and children start following you, it feels like a mob.

The most unnerving part, however, was that the leader of this gang was my own flesh and blood.

Tristan pointed and cried, "That's not Santa! That's my dad!"

I was raising Judas.

Running in that crappy Santa suit wasn't the best option, but I didn't have a lot of options, so I ran. I ran as hard as I could to the church office. I slipped and fell twice, and on the second fall, I did something to my knee, forcing me to hobble the last few feet to the office as the children gained on me. Were I an older, fatter, traditional Santa, I'd probably have broken something, and that mob of children surely would have overtaken me and stripped me of my beard and wig—and possibly my life.

I was shutting the office door when Tristan wedged his little torso inside and said in his own husky Batman voice, "I know that's you, Dad."

It felt like I'd been caught in the middle of a murder.

Tristan's gang of Santa skeptics, all varying ages, all children of my friends, crowded around the door, and I had no other option but to grab Tristan by the front of his shirt, yank him into the office, and slam the door. I turned out the lights and sat on the floor, my back against the door, children banging on the other side of it.

I was breathing heavily.

I was sweating.

Tristan just stood there and stared at me with squinted eyes, his hands in his pockets.

I sat there for some time, wondering what should happen next. I always assumed he'd find out the truth, but I never thought it'd be like this.

I shifted the pillows in my shirt and my bells jingled.

"I know it's you, Dad," he said again, only this time in a whisper.

I took a breath and removed my beard and wig.

I patted the carpet, and Tristan sat down next to me. Before I had a chance to say anything, he let out a long breath and said, "I've known for a while."

I asked him why he told his mother and me he still believed in Santa, and he said, "I don't know." In a way, it felt like what he was really saying was, "I still wanted to believe."

It was quiet.

The kids outside had moved on.

This Santa thing hadn't gone the way I expected. No doubt about it. In fact, it was a pretty big fail. Particularly when you consider I had to see a doctor about my knee. But there was something about this moment in the church office, me partially dressed like Santa, Tristan crouching next to me, that actually felt like a Norman Rockwell painting—our version of it, anyway.

I put my arm around Tristan and said, "Well, the gig's up." I blew some air between my lips. Then I said, "Now that you're in on the secret, you want to start helping with Christmas?"

He gave me the same hangdog look he always gave me when I asked him to do something around the house.

"It's not like that," I said.

I told him he could help us move the elf and fill the stockings.

"It's pretty fun," I said. "And you get to stay up late."

He smiled as I spoke, and I told him he could help only if he didn't say a word to his sisters. He smiled even bigger then, and I could tell he felt like he was in on something truly special.

YOU CAN'T FORCE
A TRADITION

The day after Thanksgiving, we went into the Oregon woods and cut down a Christmas tree. Actually, wait. Perhaps "into the Oregon woods" was misleading. We didn't wander deep into the woods, hiking through knee-deep snow to find the perfect tree like Clark Griswold and his family did in *Christmas Vacation*. Instead we drove to a tree farm twenty minutes from our house. It was one of those places where, usually less than a quarter of a mile from our van, you pick out a tree as a family and cut it down yourself, similar to visiting a pumpkin patch.

I got to use a saw and rope. I put on boots and coveralls and I wore real leather gloves. I brought my own bow saw. Visiting the tree farm was our family tradition and had been ever since we moved to Oregon six years earlier.

Cutting down our own tree was one of the few opportunities I had to really shine as a father. I don't have a lot of memories like that with my own dad. He walked out shortly after my ninth birthday.

He was in and out of jail for drug addiction most of my teen years, and he died just before his 50th birthday. His absence made me feel like I was missing something as a father, because I didn't have a great example growing up. That's the reason I named my blog No Idea What I'm Doing.

One thing I do know for sure about Dad: He could do a lot of handy, fix-it-up things. He showed my older brothers how to do that stuff before he left, but he didn't teach me because I was too young. I've always hated that I never had those heartwarming, working-with-your-hands moments with my dad. I always want to create those moments with my own children, but don't really know how.

TO PUT THIS INTO PERSPECTIVE, I ONCE CHANGED THE BATTERY IN OUR FAMILY VAN AND IT TOOK ME TWO HOURS. AND TO SAY THAT IT TOOK ME TWO HOURS MAKES IT SOUND LIKE I SUCCESSFULLY CHANGED THE BATTERY, WHICH IS UNTRUE.

I'm pretty bad at fixing things, and cutting things, and saving money by doing things myself. I didn't learn any of that from my dad, and I obviously haven't been very good at figuring it out myself. To put this into perspective, I once changed the battery in our family van and it took me two hours. And to say that it took me two hours makes it sound like I successfully changed the battery, which is untrue. Well, it's roughly 50 percent true, because I did get the battery connected, and it worked for three weeks or so—but eventually we were left stranded on a dark stretch of rural highway, all of it feeling like *The Texas Chainsaw Massacre*. I had the van towed to a mechanic, who laughed at me because I'd stripped the bolts on the cables, so they fell off when we drove over a bump. Blah, blah, blah . . . the story of me working with my hands up to this point. Replace "car battery" with "door," "sink," "toilet," "shelving unit," "doorknob," "sports," "turkey carving," or "power tools" and you'll get the same story.

But I was pretty good at cutting down a Christmas tree, and that felt significant for some reason. It felt like a way to give my children one of those moments I never had with my own father, so that my kids would look back on their childhood with bright-eyed warmth, smile, and say, "That was my papa!"

I had something special planned for this year. I was going to have Tristan, my twelve-year-old son, cut down the tree. I hoped to do the same thing with all of my children, but he was the oldest, and this all seemed like a very nice father-and-child moment that we'd both remember forever and ever and one day tell the grandkids about. Perhaps he'd do the same thing with his children, and that felt pretty special too. Like I was passing on something significant.

I was pretty darn excited, which was in complete contrast with how Tristan felt. He viewed this outing as a waste of his valuable time, which I found ironic considering no one outside of me had ever paid him for his time (and that going rate was well below minimum wage).

DURING THIS TIME OF YEAR, I USUALLY GAUGED THE HORRIBLENESS OF OUTINGS BY HOW MANY TIMES I HAD TO CANCEL CHRISTMAS.

He fought with Aspen and Norah on the drive to the tree farm over who knows what. Mel and I spent most of the drive settling arguments and canceling Christmas.

During this time of year, I usually gauged the horribleness of outings by how many times I had to cancel Christmas. Our all-time high was at a Nativity festival. My kids thought it was funny to steal Baby Jesus out of different mangers. I kept canceling Christmas to get Baby Jesus back. The grand total was five cancellations. That's five stolen Baby Jesuses, which I'm confident equals eternal damnation.

Anyway, by the time we made it to the tree farm, I'd already canceled Christmas three times, and Mel and I were glassy-eyed and tired. It's funny: We had multiple kids with the understanding that they would play together. But what they did do didn't sound like play at all.

It sounded like attempted murder.

Tristan was technically a preteen, a title synonymous with bottomless pit. All the kid did was eat. It was insane. Full moon: "I'm hungry." No moon: "I'm hungry." Partly cloudy: "I'm hungry." Apocalypse: "Can we pleeeease go to KFC?"

It didn't matter the day, time, weather, or lunar calendar—he was hungry.

Tristan stopped talking about how hungry he was so he could tell me he was cold. Then he moved on to how he didn't want to walk anymore, despite the fact that we hadn't actually started walking. Pretty soon, it was back to, "I'm hungry . . ."

I looked him in the eyes and said, "Come on, buddy. This is our tradition. It's important."

He was wearing black track pants, a blue zippered jacket with finger-shaped oil stains across the front, and a black ball cap on backward. His greasy, shaggy brown hair shot out from beneath the cap.

He rolled his eyes. We walked between the trees. It was late in the day, almost dusk, the sun setting in oranges and blues. Mountains and hills stretched around us. The trees were heavy with snow. It smelled like pine and sawdust and mud. Everything about this moment, from the sunset to the trees, was picturesque as only Oregon can be . . . except for my daughters yelling at each other and my son dragging his feet and complaining about how stupid this whole thing was.

I don't know if this means kids ruin everything. I don't want to say that outright. But what I *will* say is that up to this moment, everything had gone according to plan except for my children.

You do the math.

I remember watching *Christmas Vacation* as a child and feeling like Clark was overemotional, but each year I better understand that scene where he freaked out and asked for the TYLENOL®.

I DON'T KNOW IF THIS MEANS KIDS RUIN EVERYTHING. I DON'T WANT TO SAY THAT OUTRIGHT. BUT WHAT I *WILL* SAY IS THAT UP TO THIS MOMENT, EVERYTHING HAD GONE ACCORDING TO PLAN EXCEPT FOR MY CHILDREN.

But I wasn't going to let Tristan's bad attitude bring me down. I strutted between the trees in my coveralls and gloves, carrying the bow saw in one hand and pinching branches with the other as if I were some sort of Christmas tree expert. I kept glancing at Tristan, curious if he was noticing all my fatherly glory. Instead he just looked at the ground, his feet dragging in the mud.

Some tree farm helpers drove by on a four-wheeler with a trailer and a chainsaw. They asked if we needed help, and I put up my hand and said, "I'm good," like I was that one guy at the hardware store who actually knew what he was doing.

Tristan looked at me and I winked, confident that he'd be impressed. But he wasn't. Not even a little bit. Instead he rolled his eyes again and said, "Why didn't you let those guys help? It would have made this go faster."

I told him how we didn't need this to go faster, and how this was our family tradition, and how we needed to savor this moment because we didn't have all that many left to share as a family. Then I asked him to hold the saw. I even held it out to him, my right hand on the handle, my left open and placed along the blade, almost like I was handing him Excalibur. He looked me up and down, his face all scrunched. I might as well have been offering him a hot turd.

"When I was your age, I'd have loved it if my dad had asked me to hold a saw," I said.

"Fine," he said in a lackluster tone that actually meant, "Can we get this over with?"

He reluctantly pulled his little hand out of his scrubby track pants, and I handed him the saw. It hung heavily at his side.

He dragged his feet and complained some more, and by the time we finally found a tree the whole family could agree on, I was ready to bury him in the Oregon woods.

I crouched down on my hands and knees and lifted up some of the tree's lower branches. He tried to hand me the saw, and I asked him to crouch down next to me.

"Why?" he asked.

"Because I want you to cut down the tree this year." I smiled up at my son, a twinkle in my eye. My face, my body, every fatherly part of me seemed to say, "This is your moment, son!"

He didn't smile back. He didn't seize the moment or look at me with admiration or excitement. Instead he took two steps back. His body went limp, his shoulders slumped at his side, and, I swear to you, he glared at me like he was Ebenezer Scrooge and I'd asked him to give Bob Cratchit a living wage. "You want me to do what?" he exclaimed.

It felt like I'd asked him to build his own house, or move a mountain, or fight a bear.

This wasn't at all how I'd pictured this moment. Not that anything he was doing was atypical preteen behavior. On the whole, Tristan was a pretty good kid. He was faithful to help with his younger sisters, and he did well in school. He had loads of friends and all of his teachers seemed to enjoy him in class. He just didn't want to do stuff that he didn't want to do, and apparently cutting down a Christmas tree was somewhere near the bottom of his list of interests, probably between eating vegetables and being kicked in the crotch.

Not that this changed my urgency to get him to help cut down the tree. I asked him again. We fought over it for a moment. At one point I told him that cutting down the tree would be a very special moment for us, and how I never got moments like this with my father, so it was important that he and I had them. He gave me a confused look and said, "What is wrong with you?"

Finally, he took a couple of swaths with the saw and then somehow ended up sitting on me as I lay on my side, cutting down the tree, while he held up the branches so I could see.

As I worked the saw, my son sitting on top of me, I couldn't help but realize how badly I sucked at traditions. I was obviously trying to force something, which never works. But if I've learned anything about being a father who grew up with an absent father, it's that it often feels like I'm getting those rewarding family moments I always wanted as a child—I'm just on the opposite end of the equation now. But sometimes that causes me to try too hard to get it just right. This was one of those times.

Once the tree fell, Tristan had this look of relief, like it was finally over. Until I asked him to haul one side of it. "Come on, bud, I could use your help here."

I don't know if it was the look of insistence on my face, or if his hunger pains had returned, but he actually grabbed the top of the tree with little argument.

We walked in a line, hauling the tree together, me leading the way. We were halfway to the van when I turned to say something fatherly like, "Teamwork makes the dream work," and I threw out my back.

It was this hot, biting pain that shot up the right side of my body and made my toes go a little numb.

Mel was off with the girls taking pictures, well out of shouting range. We still had a good 50 yards to the van. None of the farmworkers were around. I was hunched over with my hand on my back, struggling to breathe, like some 85-year-old man.

"What happened?" Tristan asked.

"Nothing," I said. "Just give me a minute." I tried to walk it off, but I could hardly move. I hobbled around for a moment. Then I bent over to pick up the tree, but it wasn't happening. The pain was far too sharp, and I had to bite my lip to keep my eyes from watering.

Tristan let out this breath that wasn't irritated, or annoyed, or anything I'd come to expect from him in the past year. It was this tone that was weighted with a sense of duty. He put his hand on my shoulder and said, "I got this, Dad."

He picked up the tree and started dragging it to the van. Mel and I both stand just over 5 feet tall, so our children might as well live at the North Pole and make toys. And indeed, at school they call Tristan "Little T" for a reason. He was the kid in class who had to stand on a box during the Christmas program.

I was surprised he could move the tree himself. And I wouldn't say that he just lifted it over his head with gusto. It looked like he was dragging a body. But outside of a few stops along the way to readjust his grip, he made it all the way to the van, me hobbling behind him, hunched over, saw in hand.

With the help of one of the farmhands, Tristan was able to get the tree on top of the van. Then he threw some rope over the top and tied the knots I'd fought with him to learn each and every year. They weren't perfect, but it seemed clear that they would hold.

As the family reconvened by the van, with the tree strapped to the top and me sitting on the driver's side, my feet on the ground and my hand on my back, Tristan approached me while dusting his hands and said, "That wasn't too hard."

It was something I'd said every year after cutting down a Christmas tree, and he always rolled his eyes. I wanted to say one of those dad comments about how someone must have replaced my son, but I didn't want to produce another eye roll. I'd had my quota for the day.

But I must say, I couldn't help but realize that he'd actually been paying attention each year, and I had this warm feeling that someday he'd be teaching his children how to cut down a tree.

"Thanks, bud," I said.

He smiled.

"Are you going to help me haul it into the house?"

He swelled his chest a little and said, "Yeah, Dad. I got you."

WHEN THE KIDS HAVE A SNOW DAY YOU CAN BET I'LL BE DOING SOMETHING STUPID

I don't know why I toss my young children into the air way, way, higher than any child should ever be tossed, only to catch them moments before they crash to the ground. I don't know why I wrestle with them in the living room, or creep up below them at the swimming pool, grab one leg, and then lift them into the air as though I'd caught some massive two-legged fish. But the worst of all is when it snows. I swear, the ground goes white, we all get a little bored, and it's like the light of the full moon hitting a werewolf.

Here are a few examples.

I tossed my son into a pile of snow only for him to sink to the bottom.

During a snowstorm on Christmas Eve, I took three-year-old Tristan outside to play in the snow. I playfully tossed him into a snowdrift. When I was young and my dad did this, I laughed and thought it was awesome. When I did it with Tristan, he sank to the bottom of the drift as if I'd tossed him into the ocean. Understandably, I freaked the eff out and then dug through several feet of snow to find my son coated in white. He coughed up a snowy, drooly slush, and then he looked up at me with the sweetest blue eyes and said, "Why did you do that, Daddy?" I didn't have a good answer. I told him I was sorry, brought him inside for some hot cocoa, and let him open one of his Christmas presents.

I accidentally hit my daughter in the face with a snowball.

When Norah was six, she threw a snowball at me, so I threw one back. Only, in true dad form, I accidentally hit her right in the face. She cried. She cried long and hard and looked at me like I was a huge jerk. Which, I will admit, hitting a six-year-old in the face with a snowball is a jerk thing to do. However, in my defense, when it comes to throwing snowballs, I'm like a *Star Wars* stormtrooper: Ninety-nine percent of the time, I miss the person entirely. The fact that I actually hit Norah was an incredible stroke of bad luck. Norah ended up with some bruising along her cheek, and now every time someone sees the Christmas card from that year I get to explain that I hit my daughter in the face with a snowball. I always say it was an accident, because it was. And they always look at me as if I'm a jerk-face—which, considering the situation, may actually be true.

I went off a snow jump on a sled with my son and landed in a parking lot.

We went sledding on Christmas Eve, and there was this awesome jump at the bottom of one of the hills. Listen, I'm not going to say that I intentionally went off the jump with Tristan, then five years old, on my lap. But what I will say is that I didn't exactly try to avoid it because I thought, *It'd be pretty cool if we went off that sucker.* Does this make me a bad father? I hope not. I think it just makes me the kind of dad that's up for adventure— someone similar to Indiana Jones, but without Nazis. Between the ice and the pitch of the jump, we got some pretty epic air and ended up landing in the freshly plowed parking lot, which is a lot harder than snow. You can trust me on that. On a positive note, I landed in the parking lot, and Tristan landed on me. He cried because he was scared. I know this because I broke his fall with my face. I rolled around on the ground, attempting to get the wind back in my body as he cried. But I would like it to be known that once I could finally breathe again, and Tristan had stopped crying, he asked if we could do it again.

"Maybe," I said.

My kids made a snow angel and found dog poop. I have to assume this is self-explanatory. I went to the backyard with the kids to make snow angels. And, yes, under the snow was dog poop. It was nasty, but the real question is: Who is to blame for this? I'd love to blame God, or fate or just plain old bad luck. I'd really love to blame the dog, but he is entitled to poop the same as anyone. To be honest, it was my fault. I was asked repeatedly to pick up after the dog before it snowed. And I kept saying, "I'll get to it." Same as I do with the burned-out bulbs in the hallway and the batteries in the smoke alarms. I swear, if I died today, Mel would summon me with a Ouija board just to say, "Before you died, you forgot to change the lightbulbs above the sink. But don't worry . . . *I got it!*"

I just didn't expect it to snow in Oregon that year. But then, bam! It did, and two out of three kids came in the house after making snow angels with dog poop up their backs. Then they unwittingly sat on the sofa, as kids often do, without inspecting themselves for poop, and I ended up spending my Christmas vacation shampooing the sofa and gagging and cursing my own laziness.

I drove 45 minutes to find snow only for my daughter to cry the whole time.

Did I want to drive 45 minutes to have a snowball fight? No. Not really. But Aspen did, and it was our Saturday to do whatever she wanted, and when she looked up at me with those crazy-excited eyes that only a five-year-old can get, I had no doubt that it was snow or nothing.

So we drove into the mountains until we found just enough snow. She cried as I fought her little fingers into gloves, the whole time wondering how I had finished college yet still struggled with kids' gloves. We built a little snowman, and then she cried when its head exploded as I tried to give it a carrot nose. I threw the first snowball, and she cried and accused me of cheating. According to Aspen, only she could throw snow in a snowball fight, which I felt was terribly one-sided. Then she hit me in the neck with a massive, muddy wad of snow and laughed as I dug snow out of my shirt, reminding me of that grade-school bully who used to do the exact same thing but who also punched me in the butt cheek, making it go numb for a couple of hours. She cried one last time when she slipped and fell on her face.

We were there for twenty minutes, which felt like a lot of driving for a lot of crying. We drove back home and got some hot cocoa, and as we sat there sipping I assumed this whole event was a bust. Then she looked at me and asked to do it again next weekend. I reminded her that she cried the whole time, and she reached across the table, her fingers still a little pink from the cold, took my hand, and let out a breath that seemed to say, "You just don't get it."

Then she said, "Sometimes snow makes me cry."

"But you still like it?" I asked.

She nodded excitedly.

I may never fully understand my children. . . .

You know, for the sake of my children, it's probably best that we now live in a very safe part of Oregon where it almost never snows.

I'M AS SURPRISED AS MY CHILDREN BY WHAT I GOT THEM FOR CHRISTMAS

A week before Thanksgiving, Mel asked me to read something from her phone: "I'm excited for Christmas morning, to see the look of surprise on my husband's face when he finds out what he bought for everyone."

She didn't smile, or laugh, or say another word. She just stared at me with the subtlety of a Molotov cocktail, phone still in her hand, and I got the feeling that what I'd just read was something she'd wanted to say for years but that she'd never had the right words for.

I was doing dishes at the time. She was in gray leggings, an old gray university T-shirt, and fuzzy, bright-colored slippers. Our three children were upstairs for the night.

I'd seen this viral meme several times leading up to Christmas. I laughed reading it each time while thinking about all those other dads that didn't have their acts together. Those fathers had Christmas preparation problems, while I was an advanced, modern feminist father.

Perhaps I should admit that I was a little full of myself during this time. Not that I walked into grocery stores and screamed, "I am the best father in the history of fathers! Bring me all the fathers so they can learn at my feet!" But my ego was pretty inflated. I'd had a number of posts go viral that year. Thousands (in some cases millions) of women tagged the heck out of the men in their lives, all of them unanimously saying, "Be like this dad."

I was feeling a little too good about who I was as a husband and father.

To make matters even more complicated, the meme Mel read was written by Joelle Wisler, who worked with me as a staff writer at Scary Mommy. I got a little defensive. Okay, maybe "little" isn't a strong enough word. Perhaps a better adverb would be "very" or "extremely" or "over-the-top douchebag."

I accused Mel of making me out to be one of those bumbling Homer Simpson–type dads. "Don't put me in that category," I said. "I'm a good dad. I have a dad blog. I write books about being a good dad. I'm reflective." I went on, listing all of my fatherly credentials as if I were defending my position in some sort of a professional review. I even went as far as to mention that time one of my articles was discussed on the *TODAY* show and Kathie Lee Gifford said I seemed like a pretty nice dad. "How many fathers do you know who have an endorsement from Kathie Lee Gifford?" I asked.

Mel didn't agree with me. She didn't back down. She just asked me a very simple question: "What are you getting the kids for Christmas this year?"

Silence.

I thought.

I made a few false starts.

I stammered.

I thought some more.

"HOW MANY FATHERS DO YOU KNOW WHO HAVE AN ENDORSEMENT FROM KATHIE LEE GIFFORD?" I ASKED.

I had a loose idea . . . didn't I? We were getting that one thing . . . with the fur . . . that talks . . . what was it called? Or did we decide not to get that because it was too expensive? There was also that puppy that made burp sounds, and that video game thingy with the blocks and that guy named Steve. What was it called?

As I gave vague descriptions of toys I remembered my children asking for but couldn't remember the details, Mel grabbed my bicep and pulled me to the kitchen table as my hands still dripped from loading the dishwasher. She sat down and opened her laptop. She clicked on a few things and then said, "Here! This is what 'you'"—she made air quotes with her fingers—"are getting the kids for Christmas."

On her computer was a comprehensive spreadsheet. It listed all the things the kids wanted. She ranked them. She had price comparisons. To the right was a budget of how much we had for each child. Behind the spreadsheet I could see windows on her browser stretching into the eternities, full of toys and clothes and books. She had a column with short reviews for each product, along with a pretty robust color code. As much as I didn't want to admit it, her spreadsheet was epic.

Mel turned and looked at me with these bloodshot eyes that only a mother has around Christmastime.

"See?" Mel said with a satisfied smirk. "You have no idea what you are getting the kids for Christmas. You know why? Because I do all the Christmas. All of it. Every inch of Christmas." As she spoke, she poked herself in the chest.

About a year after my parents' divorce, on Christmas Day, my father gave my brother and I each a wadded-up handful of cash, without a card, in an exchange that I imagine felt pretty similar to how he paid for drugs. At the time I was like, "Sweet! I'm buying a moped!" But then I counted it and realized it was only about $30 in ones and fives. Now I realize that he completely forgot to get me anything, and this was his last-ditch effort to do something. Sadly, however, if Christmas were suddenly on my shoulders, I'd have ended up doing the same thing, and Mel's spreadsheet only proved that. Although I knew it, as I look back at this moment, I wasn't ready to admit it.

The logical part of my brain came to that conclusion, and it was at battle with what I call my pride center. That's the part of my brain that just doesn't want to relent and acknowledge that I was wrong, so I argued some more, bringing up how we went shopping last year at Target and how we bought a whole cart full of stuff for Christmas.

And you know what Mel did? She scoffed. Right in my face. Then she cocked her head back and laughed, and it felt like that time our son announced he could live on his own after learning how to make pancakes.

Then she said, "If you think our Christmas shopping is done with one trip to Target, then I assume you still believe in Santa Claus."

We went to bed that night without speaking, our backs to each other. I couldn't sleep. I lay awake and thought about the year before, when I sat next to the tree at five o'clock in the morning, half awake, watching the kids open their gifts with a sense of wonder. I was so excited to see what they got. I was as giddy with anticipation as they were, unsure of what was hidden inside the wrapping paper. It almost felt like Santa had come. The year before that, and the year before that, all the way back to that first Christmas we shared with our newborn son, were the same.

WHO WAS REALLY MAKING THE MAGIC? NOT THIS FAT AND JOLLY OLD MAN, NO SIR. IT WAS MY WIFE.

For the first time in my fatherly life, I accepted the fact that I sucked at planning Christmas, and I couldn't help but wonder how I got here. It wasn't intentional. I didn't set out to do less or take advantage of Mel. The more I thought, the more I realized it was a mix of things. Mel was fantastic at planning, and organizing, and buying stuff (see epic spreadsheet example on page 85), so I just stayed in my lane and let her run with this whole Christmas thing. As we had more kids, she kept at it. I didn't want to get in the way, which in a lot of ways meant I just didn't get involved. And sure, I knew she was doing all the Christmas work, but I didn't fully realize how much work that actually was. Or perhaps I should say I didn't take the time to find out how much work went into our Christmas preparation. All of these things added up to her working tirelessly into the night planning Christmas for our children while I put on blinders, going to work and to bed at my usual times, not giving the whole ordeal much thought. Come Christmas morning, I'd take half the credit for the magic of Christmas without a second thought.

Sure, it took us years to get to the point where Mel did all the Christmas preparation—and my lack of help didn't stem from malice—but the fact remained that I called myself Santa on Christmas Eve. Who was really making the magic? Not this fat and jolly old man, no sir.

It was my wife.

Nothing I've mentioned so far made me an exceptional father or husband. It was actually a huge slap in the face to my wife each year.

I couldn't help but wonder why she hadn't brought this to my attention sooner, but to be honest, maybe she had and I just hadn't been listening. I mean, come on, she'd been planning Christmas for years and I hadn't noticed that.

Anyway, after pondering on this for a good amount of time, I started to feel pretty low. I finally relented and admitted to myself, God, and everyone that I had not been putting my whole heart into this Christmas-planning thing each year and I needed to step it up.

By morning, after sleeping only a few hours, Mel and I sat across from each other eating breakfast, our children watching TV in the living room. There are a few phrases that all wives love to hear from their husband: "I love you," "You are important to me," "I value your contributions." But the two phrases that they love the most are what I said in that moment.

"You're right," I said. "I'm sorry."

Mel graciously accepted my apology. Then she opened the door and invited me into her world of holiday pain.

The next several nights, we stayed up late discussing toys and trying to figure out what was going to work for our kiddos. On Black Friday we sat side by side on the sofa, ordering things online, discussing deals and our budget and trying to find the right gifts for our children.

We talked a lot about Christmas. And I will admit, during this time, I often commended her on her ability to organize. I told her how amazing she was and how much I appreciated her doing all of this for so many years. I apologized for not noticing it sooner. I gained an incredible admiration for Mel and her Christmastime contributions.

However, that being said, I will also say that I'm surprised we made it all the way to Christmas without Mel putting bars of soap in a pillowcase and beating me to death. And to be fair, I felt the same about her.

She had a pretty particular idea of how things ought to go, and I wasn't exactly getting in line. Not that I was doing anything wrong, mind you. My heart was in the right place. I wanted to pull my Christmas-planning weight, but I had my own ways of doing things.

I asked a lot of obvious questions, and I messed up our Christmas budget a number of times by buying things that weren't on the list but that I felt were worth the extra money because they were "awesome!" One night we got into a heated argument while trying to pick out a shirt for our son. Mel thought he'd really like a *Harry Potter* T-shirt boasting the cover of his favorite book from the series, while I was 100 percent sure he'd rather have a soccer shirt.

The *Harry Potter* shirt arrived the day before Christmas. As I was wrapping it, I brought up the argument again, because I'm an idiot.

Out of frustration and stress and who knows what else, Mel blurted, "You know what, it was a lot easier to do this before you got involved!"

I was hunched down on the floor next to the tree, wrapping paper in hand. I realized it was one of those moments we have from time to time, where my trying to pitch in was actually making things harder—kind of like every time I began the bedtime routine with a wrestling match.

It was quiet for some time.

Then I finally asked, "I thought you wanted me to be involved here?"

"Well . . . yes," she responded. "I did. But now I'm not sure." She put her face in her hands. "I mean, I've done this on my own. What really bothered me was what you were missing out on each year."

"What do you mean?" I asked.

"Forget it," she said.

And once again, we went to bed without speaking.

And once again, I couldn't sleep.

I thought about how I learned that Tristan asked for a shirt with a cat in space shooting lightning from its paws while eating a pizza and I actually scratched a hole in my head trying to understand. I marveled that his wish list added up to just over $5,000 worth of game systems and game downloads and some advanced gaming mouse for our family computer, and I'd never wanted to make him live on the streets until then.

AND AS IF HAVING A DOG HER FATHER DISLIKED WASN'T ENOUGH, ASPEN ASKED FOR A STUFFED DOG THAT LICKED AND TWERKED AND . . .

Norah and Aspen asked for a Barbie® Dream-House™ to share so they could fight over a pretend house inside our real house. And as if having a dog her father disliked wasn't enough, Aspen asked for a stuffed dog that licked and twerked along with a walking unicorn who declared its love, and suddenly I wondered if Christmas morning was going to be like Narnia meets Miley Cyrus.

Norah asked for a bath bomb maker, a child-sized foot massager, and a children's press-on nail kit, making me feel like I was raising Paris Hilton. YouTube had somehow convinced her that everything should come in a magic egg, and those eggs cost as much as $60, and knowing that made me want to die.

And as I thought, I realized I understood my children well enough to wonder if they needed therapy. But I obviously didn't have money for that sort of thing because it was all being spent on magic eggs.

NORAH ASKED FOR A BATH BOMB MAKER, A CHILD-SIZED FOOT MASSAGER, AND A CHILDREN'S PRESS-ON NAIL KIT, MAKING ME FEEL LIKE I WAS RAISING PARIS HILTON.

The real kicker, though, came that Christmas morning. There were no surprises. I knew exactly what my children were getting. I knew why they wanted it, and what it meant to them. Each and every gift had thought and love and compassion behind it. I knew how much it cost, and I knew exactly why we bought it.

I felt warmth in my chest that morning I'd never felt on any previous Christmas morning. As I looked at my family enjoying themselves— the scene similar to what I'd experienced in the years previously, but somehow weightier with emotion—I realized what I'd been missing each and every year by not being more involved. I missed out on all the wonderful behind-the-scenes planning, and the feeling that comes along with orchestrating a perfect Christmas morning, not just witnessing it.

Mel was sitting on our sofa, and I was leaning against the wall next to the tree, holding a black garbage bag full of used wrapping paper. Between us was a sea of toys. She gave me this raised-eyebrow look that seemed to say, "See?"

I smiled and nodded.

SOMETIMES ON NEW YEAR'S EVE, YOU FIND POOP IN YOUR HALLWAY

It was close to 2:00 a.m. on New Year's Eve. Or was it New Year's Day now? Regardless, finding a turd in your hallway was a horrible way to celebrate the New Year.

This was an hour after closing shop on a New Year's Eve party for my children. I'd like to say we had a real bender, but we're Mormons, so it was more of a "let's try to make the most of New Year's Eve by inviting some friends over and watching kids' movies" situation. Which, by definition, isn't a bender unless you are in sixth grade.

But come on. How much fun is New Year's for someone who doesn't drink?

That's a good question, and I'll answer it: not that fun. This was actually the first year I'd stayed up past 10:00 p.m. on New Year's Eve in a long time, because I just didn't see the point. Sure, the kids asked to stay up later, and some years Mel stayed up with them because she's cool like that. But I always went to bed well before midnight.

BUT COME ON. HOW MUCH FUN IS NEW YEAR'S FOR SOMEONE WHO DOESN'T DRINK? THAT'S A GOOD QUESTION, AND I'LL ANSWER IT: NOT THAT FUN.

There are a number of holidays that I look forward to. Christmas, for example. I love me some Christmas. The Fourth of July, because I love me some fireworks. I really enjoy Halloween because candy is the cornerstone of my diet, and I love that I can eat it guilt-free while also wearing a costume that masks my dad bod.

But I did not look forward to New Year's Eve. It was my least favorite holiday since I stopped drinking.

And sure, I'd been sober for well over a decade by this time. And yes, I was comfortable with not drinking. And no, I was never an alcoholic or anything. But there was a time I enjoyed getting a little loopy on New Year's Eve because, you know, that's what you do.

And when I piled it all up—kids, house payment, full-time job, minivan, Costco pants, sobriety, Mormonism—I felt like a pretty big nerd. And, to be real, I was. I still am. A few weeks ago, I was shopping on AMBIEN® . . . apparently. I found out the morning after that I bought two shirts. One portrayed the cover of Mary Shelley's *Frankenstein*, the other the cover of *The Hound of the Baskervilles* (my favorite Sherlock Holmes book). Even when I'm high on sleeping pills, I'm a complete nerd. But I think trying to overcome all those nerdy feelings was what this New Year's Eve party was all about.

AND WHEN I PILED IT ALL UP—KIDS, HOUSE PAYMENT, FULL-TIME JOB, MINIVAN, COSTCO PANTS, SOBRIETY, MORMONISM—I FELT LIKE A PRETTY BIG NERD.

I was trying to prove to myself that I could still cut loose on New Year's Eve despite being a four-alarm nerdy Mormon father and husband.

But I don't think anything could have made me feel like a bigger loser than cleaning up a turd on my hallway floor in the wee hours of New Year's Day.

Our stand-up, full-sized traditional carpet shampooer was broken, so I used the handheld spot cleaner, which meant I had to get really close to the turd. And as I started scrubbing, I couldn't help but think about the fact that this was some unrelated-to-me child's poop. Something about that realization turned my stomach, and I'm not sure why. Poop really should be poop, regardless of whose butt it came from. But that isn't true. There's something desensitizing about your own child's poop. I handled their turds so many times it felt like a job, the same as doing the laundry or dishes or some other disagreeable but ultimately banal part of parenting. But knowing that it was some other child's poop in my hallway made it downright nasty.

I gagged as I scrubbed it out of the carpet. Then, as I washed the hand scrubber's tank, I had a different feeling: a sickening feeling of being walked on, kind of like when you're the nerd in school, and you've been doing homework for some cool jock, and suddenly you realize that he's not actually your friend.

He's just using you.

I don't want to use their real last name, so I'll just call them the Butthole Faces. Yes, that sounds accurate. The Butthole Faces from We-Took-Advantage-of-Clint-on-New-Year's-Eve-Ville.

They were friends of ours. Were. I invited them over to watch movies and eat pizza and play games. I told them that our kids could play while we talked, and they were all about it until I mentioned that I wouldn't be serving alcohol.

The conversation went like this:

"Yeah, that sounds awesome. What kind of booze will you be serving?"

"We don't really do that at our house, but we can still have a good time. We'll have chips and pizza. We can watch movies and maybe even play Toy Story Yahtzee® Jr.!"

Silence.

"Hey, hello? You still there?"

Silence.

It's funny, when I look back at that conversation, I probably sounded like Napoleon Dynamite, which is a fair assessment. We did serve tater tots at the party, but even Napoleon deserves more respect than what I received.

After a very long pause, Mr. Butthole Face said, "How do you feel about just watching our kids on New Year's Eve?"

WAS I PATHETIC? I DON'T KNOW. PROBABLY? I MEAN, I DON'T WANT TO AGREE TO THAT TITLE, BUT LOOKING AT THE SITUATION, IT SURE APPEARS THAT WAY.

I'll say it: This was a dick move on his part. Up to this point we'd been decent friends. Not super close, but I liked the guy. All of our kids got along wonderfully, and that says a lot. Mel also got along with Mrs. Butthole Face, which was nice. Up until that moment, I felt good about inviting them. But wow. Who gets invited to a party and then turns it around to, "How about you watch our kids while we go out drinking on New Year's?" These people obviously saw me as the nerdy, overly nice type that would change his plans and become the sitter while they drank.

So you know what I did?

I'll tell you!

I folded like a taco and agreed to watch all of the children because I'm a really nice guy who can't seem to say no or recognize when I'm being walked on.

We took all four of the Butthole Face children into our home on New Year's Eve. We had pizza and candy. We played *Pokémon* while Mr. and Mrs. Butthole Face went out drinking.

I was the designated parent, watching other people's kids because they all knew I was the sober religious type that could be trusted to watch children.

Was I pathetic?

I don't know. Probably? I mean, I don't want to agree to that title, but looking at the situation, it sure appears that way.

I tried hard to not let this turn of events bring down my plans for an awesome New Year's Eve extravaganza, so I busted loose with those kids. We broke out *Shrek* and *Shrek 2*. We broke out *The Goonies*. We played TWISTER and broke open a massive Costco bag of veggie straws. We had cupcakes and pizzas. We had a little dance party in the kitchen.

It was off the hook.

And as things were heating up around 10:30 p.m., I was feeling like a cool, classy, successful parent who threw a lit kid-friendly New Year's Eve party and was now the coolest dad on the block.

But between 11:00 p.m. and midnight, the party boat took on water. Everyone was hyped up on sugar and acting like our dog when the doorbell rings.

One child threw up in our garbage can because he ate too much pizza and candy and then jumped around on my sofa. One of the boys peed all over the toilet seat, and someone wiped their nose on my drapes. There was a lot of screaming and a lot of running, and someone broke our lamp.

ONE CHILD THREW UP IN OUR GARBAGE CAN BECAUSE HE ATE TOO MUCH PIZZA AND CANDY AND THEN JUMPED AROUND ON MY SOFA.

All of this felt like the last New Year's party I'd been to as a drinker, only I didn't have the pleasure of being drunk. And let me just say that when people are breaking your stuff and puking in your garbage can, being drunk makes all the difference.

By the time I found the turd in my hallway, the other children had gone home, my house was a mess, and I was ready to question my life up to this point. Well, maybe not my whole life, but at least my reasons for throwing that freaking party.

The turd was smeared in a long line along the baseboard, small and round, almost like a 2-inch wide strip of toothpaste. It was smudged a little on one side because someone had stepped on it.

But more than anything, that turd felt like a symbol. It felt like the last straw of being the biggest walk-on in the history of walk-ons. It seemed to represent that I was a huge nerd of a dad who would gladly allow you to poop in his hallway without repercussions.

BY THE TIME I FOUND THE TURD IN MY HALLWAY, THE OTHER CHILDREN HAD GONE HOME, MY HOUSE WAS A MESS, AND I WAS READY TO QUESTION MY LIFE UP TO THIS POINT.

I leaned down and took a sniff to make sure it was poop. I mean, I was 90 percent sure it was poop, but if it was anything other than poop, I wouldn't feel quite so walked on—that 10 percent chance seemed worth it.

It was poop.

No doubt about it.

I was half awake because I'd reached that stage in life where having to be up after 10:00 p.m. felt like a personal attack.

The sad thing is, with three kids, this was not the first time someone had pooped on our carpet. Nor would it be the last. It wasn't a regular thing. It didn't happen every day. But it happened. And I suppose that's the really strange part about having kids. I'd come to expect poop might happen at any time or place. Random poop was my default.

There were seven children in our home during that party, ranging in age from 1 to 9 years old, meaning there was a 66 percent chance that this was some other child's poop in my hallway. And although there is no way to be completely positive here, I can say that after handling gallons of my children's poop, I knew their brand, and this slick, small, snakelike turd was not on-brand. Furthermore, when it comes to other kids' poop in my house, I have a zero-tolerance policy, so 66 percent was way, way, way higher than I allowed.

I already was feeling walked on for watching the Butthole Faces' kids on New Year's Eve, having them break my stuff, and then cleaning up all their messes. I just wasn't going to handle some other kid's poop.

And sure, I agreed to this party. And yes, I take full responsibility for it. But I didn't recall anywhere in this watch-all-the-kids agreement that I'd be handling some other child's poop in my hallway. And what bothered me even more was that all but one of these kids (our one-year-old daughter, Aspen) was fully potty trained.

So I got a little crazy during the wee hours of the New Year, and I pulled out my phone to text Mr. Butthole Face about their children pooping in my hallway. Was this the new me for the New Year? Was this my way of making sure I wasn't walked on ever again?

Was I the mother-effing Terminator?

No, no. Probably closer to *Kindergarten Cop*, but it was still a vast improvement.

Or at least it was for the first minute or so, until I started to have second thoughts.

Serious question: How do you tell someone their child might have pooped in your hallway? It would feel like I was accusing him of a crime. And sure, if a grown human with all their faculties willingly pooped in my hallway, they would be charged with a crime. But with the perpetrator being a minor and all, it did feel like a gray area—one of those strange in-between legal spaces where children are allowed to do something that ought to get them locked up for a couple of years, but since they are kids, we all just live, laugh, love.

SERIOUS QUESTION: HOW DO YOU TELL SOMEONE THEIR CHILD MIGHT HAVE POOPED IN YOUR HALLWAY?

I stood in the hallway and drafted a number of texts. I asked myself questions: Would I have to get diplomatic? Rather than say, "Your child pooped in my hallway," should I should say something generic like, "Poop was found in the hallway"?

I think it is an unwritten law that parents handle their own kid's poop, but what was I expecting here? For them to zip over to my house at one o'clock on New Year's morning and clean up their kid's poop? I kind of just wanted the night, along with my friendship with these people, to be over. But I also didn't want to feel like such a walked-on loser, and I wanted these Butthole Faces to know that I wasn't going to put up with this sort of physical and metaphorical crap. But at the same time, there was still that mystery, that element of not knowing exactly who pooped in my hallway. I didn't want to go around accusing everyone when I had no forensic evidence.

Finally, I sent a diplomatic text with no proper nouns: "Might want to check butts. Found turd in the hallway." I might as well have been saying, "Mistakes were made."

About twenty minutes later, shortly after I'd finished cleaning the poop, and everyone was in bed, I received this text: "No one is claiming it here."

Not that it mattered anymore. I'd already handled it. As I read the text, I felt like this might be one of the worst situations I'd experienced as a father. I tried to be the cool dad, and now I felt like a bigger, dorkier loser than I did originally.

I went to bed that night, grumbling to myself, only for Aspen to drag me out of bed shortly after 6:00 a.m., asking for breakfast. I sat at the table, half awake, feeding her Cheerios and applesauce when Tristan came out from his room wearing yellow and blue *Pokémon* pajamas, a red and blue quilt wrapped around his shoulders and dragging behind him like he was royalty, his brown hair smashed on one side.

I didn't ask him how he slept, or if he had fun, or how he was feeling. I just sat there, swimming in my own pity.

He sat next to me, leaned his body into mine, and announced, "Last night was awesome!"

He said it like he'd just had the time of his life. Like everything he'd ever wanted had come together in that moment, and although I'd felt walked on most of that evening, it felt pretty good to have my son recognize that he'd had such an awesome time.

He looked up at me, smiled, and said something I'd never heard as a father and haven't heard since: "You're the coolest dad ever."

You know, every once in a while, my kids totally come through for me in unexpected ways, and this was exactly what I needed to hear.

Suddenly the Butthole Faces dumping off their kids, the mess in my house, and the poop in my hallway . . . none of it mattered anymore.

I put my arm around my son and said, "Thanks, buddy. I needed that."

Then he asked if we could throw another party next year, and I didn't say yes or no. I used my go-to phrase for all things related to parenting that I didn't have any intentions of actually doing but wanted to avoid a fit or argument over. "Maybe," I said. "Maybe . . ."

HOLIDAY PRO-TIPS

I've been through a few holidays with kids, so I can say with confidence that each one presents challenges, frustrations, sleep deprivation, and short moments where I somehow fall a little more in love with my children. So I put together a list of tips, tricks, and helpful observations that might just make each family holiday go a little more smoothly for you.

Thanksgiving

- With ingenuity and open-mindedness, your old maternity pants become maturkey pants!
- If you want your child to be thankful on Thanksgiving, make them mac and cheese.
- You might not win an Oscar, but acting impressed by the crappy handprint paper turkey your child made at school will ultimately keep them from needing additional therapy later in life because they found that POS in the recycling.

- Although socially unacceptable, ordering pizza on Thanksgiving can keep children from crying, parents from screaming, and your neighbors from sending the police to investigate a public disturbance. (No, I have never had the cops visit for this reason. I have, however, felt confident that they might have sent the cops if we hadn't diffused the situation with pizza. Oh, pizza, is there anything you can't do?)
- One of the best ways to bolster your own mental health is to say what you're really thankful for at Thanksgiving dinner: eight-hour school days. Your kids aren't listening to you anyway.

Christmas

- You will feel weird putting one of those large, portable panel pet yards around the Christmas tree, but once you realize that it's the only way to protect the tree from your children and your children from the tree, it eventually just becomes part of the family.
- Have your son ask your wife if the tree is straight. This will help him understand marriage.
- If Christmas movies were nonfiction, it would just be two hours of parents doing dishes on Christmas Day, so keep your standards low.
- After spending Christmas break with children, you will understand why Kevin's parents "forgot him" in *Home Alone*. I'm not saying it was right. I'm just saying I understand.

- The year your child stops begging to help decorate the tree and you have to start threatening them to help decorate the tree is the year you officially have a tween.
- Get the real tree. Your house is already sticky, so the sap doesn't really matter, and the smell will help mask the already nasty smell of children.

New Year's

- Cleaning out your children's lunch boxes early will keep you from finding that truly special New Year's Day surprise.
- Convince your children that it's actually Noon-Year's Eve. You following me?
- You might feel like getting more sleep is a great New Year's resolution, but as a parent the real path to success is to just give up sleep entirely.
- You're a parent. Just accept that 9:00 p.m. is the new midnight.
- If you put your kids to bed at midnight, they will still get up at 5:00 a.m., so regardless of alcohol consumption, you will feel hungover on New Year's Day.

Easter

- Pick up the dog poop *before* the Easter egg hunt.
- There isn't an Easter Bunny costume that won't frighten your children into not sleeping for a decade, so just avoid those fluffy devils altogether.

- If there is a candy you love and your kids hate, be sure to put that exact candy in your child's Easter basket. That way you will have plenty of treats on Easter.
- Your children will always find all the Easter eggs, but they will never find their shoes.
- If Easter has taught me anything, it's that throw-up also comes in pastels.

Halloween

- All I'm saying is if you hand out melatonin gummies instead of candy, you'll be doing the whole neighborhood a favor.
- Buying a child's Halloween costume early is a straight-up trap. They will change their mind at least three more times before Halloween, and by the time they actually commit to something else, they will have already lost half of the costume, so the store won't take it back.
- The best part of carving pumpkins is that you have something to stab as your children complain about carving pumpkins.
- I cannot understate the importance of dad-taxing your children's Halloween candy. It teaches them about everything from government overreach to the art of negotiation to the lengths their own father will go for a full-sized SNICKERS®.
- Haunted houses are cool and all, but volunteering at your child's kindergarten Halloween party is where you can find real fear.

Valentine's Day

- Writing "I like big butts" on the valentines addressed to your child's classmates will really motivate them to stop insisting that you help make valentines for their classmates.

- If you buy a box of 30 valentines for your child, but there are actually 40 students in the class, just tell them this is a VIP situation.

- If you really want to make Valentine's Day special for future parents, start legislation now to make Fun Dip an illegal substance.

- What your children actually bring home in their Valentine's Day box isn't love. It's a virus.

- Bringing your children to your Valentine's Day dinner really is just a birth control reminder to other couples.

See? I made the mistakes for you. No need to thank me. Well, okay, you can thank me.

I like feeling appreciated.

YOU HAVEN'T MACGYVERED UNTIL YOUR CHILD CRAPS THEIR PANTS IN A CORN MAZE

We were well inside the corn maze when Aspen, our two-year-old blonde wild child, squatted down next to some cornstalks, her face red, and let out a rumbling, bubbling sound that was longer and louder than I'd probably ever heard from one of our children's butts. Perhaps it was the acoustics of a corn maze. Do they have acoustics? Maybe they can make the already terrible sound of a two-year-old's anus flooding their diaper sound worse than usual. Or possibly she'd been saving this particular load for the most inconvenient time imaginable, like when her parents were well inside a corn maze. Or possibly this place was haunted, and this was the otherworld trying to speak to us through my daughter's anus.

Regardless of the reason, I was terrified.

Mel and I both let out a breath, almost in unison, and then she asked me for the diaper bag. I stared at her with neither a diaper bag nor anything that could be used to manage this situation outside of my actual hands, which is something I'd rather never do but was quickly becoming a viable option.

"I must have left it in the van," I said with this innocent shrug that I assumed was boyish and a little cute and would absolve me from doing something as stupid as forgetting the diaper bag before entering a corn maze.

I STARED AT HER WITH NEITHER A DIAPER BAG NOR ANYTHING THAT COULD BE USED TO MANAGE THIS SITUATION OUTSIDE OF MY ACTUAL HANDS, WHICH IS SOMETHING I'D RATHER NEVER DO BUT WAS QUICKLY BECOMING A VIABLE OPTION.

She approached Aspen and examined the damage. It was really something. I could tell that from where I stood. The smell was well into the "Wow!" category, and I could hear it squishing.

I suppose I should have expected Mel's reaction. She gave me those eyes mothers sometimes get, the ones that twitch a little and are terrifying and make you wonder if she'll bury you. And I must say, dumping a body in a corn maze would probably be a great place to get away with murder. Not that I've ever done something like that, but looking around at how alone and secluded we were, I have to assume she could have gotten away with it.

"*I asked you to grab the diaper bag!*" she exclaimed, as if the words were actual fire pointed at my face and it was just a matter of time before I melted completely and had to be hauled around in a plastic wheelbarrow.

"I ASKED YOU TO GRAB THE DIAPER BAG!" SHE EXCLAIMED, AS IF THE WORDS WERE ACTUAL FIRE POINTED AT MY FACE AND IT WAS JUST A MATTER OF TIME BEFORE I MELTED COMPLETELY AND HAD TO BE HAULED AROUND IN A PLASTIC WHEELBARROW.

And sure, forgetting a bag should be a forgivable offense, but until you've been a parent of a young child, you have no idea how much safety is contained in the diaper bag. It had everything, from snacks to wipes to extra clothing. Our daughter was this nonstop eating, and drooling, and pooping, and peeing little creature. She was also an opportunist who waited until the most inconvenient moment to do something horrible, like dropping a massive, frothy poop bomb in the middle of a corn maze.

We always had to be on the ready with her.

Always.

I looked at Mel for a moment, and then I thought back, way back, to when she might have asked me to grab the diaper bag. I dug around in my brain pretty far, searching and searching, but . . . nope.

Nothing.

I had nothing.

Naturally, I didn't want to say anything more because I knew it would come back to the same old argument we often had, in which she accused me of not listening. Not that I didn't listen. I totally listened . . . most of the time.

Like 90 percent.

Okay, perhaps it's more like 75 percent, but that's a pretty strong percentage. You can obtain a college degree with 75 percent—or even less—in every class and get a good job, get married, own a house, and become a father.

Trust me. I know.

But I will admit, since I'd become an Internet personality of sorts, I hadn't been a perfect listener, and I think that is what Mel and my children were looking for.

Okay, I'll come clean.

Chances are, when Mel asked me to grab the diaper bag, I was probably screwing around on my phone, answering a few messages on my blog's Facebook page. I probably nodded in that very stereotypical way I often did, pretending to listen but not actually listening with my ears.

I know this sounds like a typical twenty-first century father problem, but I will admit that I was notorious for this. Sure, it drove my wife nuts. But more importantly, it also drove my children crazy. It wasn't unusual for one of my kids to tug my phone out of my hand and say, "Daddy! Look at me!"

In my defense, this was around the time my social media following really took off, and I went from ten thousand followers to a few hundred thousand, and I felt like I was searching for every little moment I could find to manage that page. But in the grander conversation, I do think this is a big problem for most working parents. Were it not for my phone, I'd probably be shackled to some computer in an office instead of hanging out at the corn maze with my children. However, spending that time on my phone meant I always seemed to have one foot in the real world and another online—I wasn't paying full attention to work or home and I kept forgetting things like grabbing the diaper bag, setting the stage for a horrible blowout in a corn maze without provisions.

Naturally, our older kids couldn't have cared less about any of this. They started to tug at me to keep going. Mel and I were making eye contact as Tristan pulled at me, and Norah pulled at her mother. All the while, Aspen was beginning to dissolve into a toddler-poop monster.

I asked Tristan and Norah to knock it off and stand still, and they looked at me like they were ready to wander off into the cornfield on their own, probably getting lost forever and becoming the premise of a Stephen King novel.

AND SURE, COMPARING MY DAUGHTER'S BLOWOUT TO SOMETHING AS EPIC AS THE MINOTAUR SOUNDS OVER THE TOP AND ENGLISH-MAJOR NERDY, BUT UNTIL YOU'VE BEEN TRAPPED IN A CORN MAZE WITH A POOPY TODDLER WITH NO WIPES, NO CLEAN CLOTHING, NO DIAPERS— NOTHING, NADA—THEN YOU HAVE NO IDEA HOW TERRIFYING A SITUATION LIKE THIS CAN BECOME.

I thought about the diaper bag locked in the van and wondered if there was some way for me to get to it, and suddenly it felt like we were actually in the labyrinth—only the Minotaur at the center was not a half-bull human but my own daughter and her poopy butt.

And sure, comparing my daughter's blowout to something as epic as the Minotaur sounds over the top and English-major nerdy, but until you've been trapped in a corn maze with a poopy toddler with no wipes, no clean clothing, no diapers—nothing, nada—then you have no idea how terrifying a situation like this can become.

"How did you forget the diaper bag?" Mel asked.

She was in black and orange rain boots, jeans, and a cardigan. She wanted an answer. By then, Tristan and Norah were paying more attention too. They stood at Mel's sides. Norah had her hands on the hips of her unicorn printed jeans. Tristan's hands were in the pockets of his cargo shorts.

Aspen was crying now.

Everyone was waiting for an explanation.

I wanted to explain myself. I wanted to say something comforting like, "We will figure it out," or, "I'm sure it's not that bad." But as my whole family stared into my soul, waiting for me to come clean, I quickly realized that nothing I could say would prevent me from looking like a forgetful sack of garbage.

Finally I said, "So I was on my phone responding to some comments . . ."

I didn't even get it all out when all three of them let out a collective moan. Tristan went as far as to say, "Dad!"

Mel rolled her eyes.

Aspen walked up to Mel, stink lines shooting up from her body, poop visibly soaking through her day-at-the-pumpkin-patch faded jeans and up the back of her orange shirt with an adorable jack-o'-lantern on it.

"Isn't there an emergency exit in these things?" Mel asked.

This was an emergency exit sort of situation, but for the life of me, I couldn't find any signs that led to an exit. I wondered what people did when they had a health emergency in a corn maze. It's not like this was a department store. There weren't exactly employees running around giving directions.

There being zero directions was more or less the goal of the whole outing.

It was midday and cloudy, and we were in rural Oregon. I hadn't seen a single person outside of our family and a couple of scarecrows holding riddles since we entered that stupid maze. It all felt very *Alice in Wonderland.*

"Listen," I said, "we've already been walking around here for 40-something minutes. We have to be close to the end."

Not that I knew anything for sure. We'd been to this same corn maze a few times, but each year they changed the layout. I think the theme this year was *Harry Potter* or something. From the sky, it was supposed to look like a golden snitch.

Some years it took us 40 minutes and some years it took a couple of hours to make it through the maze. One year a bunch of Joe Exotic–looking drunks were going through it with us. They kept throwing corn at each other and dropping f-bombs. That was the only time I'd ever seen someone who worked at the maze actually in the maze. It was some tall, lanky farmer who kept telling the drunks they couldn't bring booze into the corn maze. They kept screaming back at him, "It's not booze! It's a beverage!" Which was almost a direct quote from Jenny Lawson, making them the most well-read hillbilly drunks ever to enter a corn maze.

I wondered if making a drunken ruckus was the only way to get someone to come help you through the maze, and I wished I'd brought some booze, or a beverage, or perhaps meth—whatever I needed to do to get some attention.

Aspen reached up for her mother, and Mel looked at me with this straight-lipped look that seemed to say, "You did this. You pick her up."

So I did, and she cried, and she smelled terrible, and I laid her down in a small patch of grass and dead cornstalks. I took off her pants, and took off her diaper, and wiped her down with some corn leaves. Is that what they were? Husks, maybe. I don't know. I've never been much into corn. Just rest assured, I was getting pretty rustic with this diaper change. Not that anything I found did much good. It felt like I was spackling drywall.

I was scratching her skin, and she was getting even fussier.

I was making a terrible mess, poop up to my wrists, some of it on my jeans, when Mel finally started to soften a little. She crouched down at my side and helped. Aspen's shirt wasn't too bad, just a small splotch of brown up the back, but her pants were a total loss, so I used what little bit of clean denim there was to wipe off her legs.

I used her socks too.

But when that wasn't enough, I ended up donating my socks as well.

The little girl looked up at Mel and I in a cornfield as we attempted to figure out how best to cover her bottom. Naturally, we considered just letting her walk around naked, hopeful that if we ran into anyone, they'd just assume people in rural Oregon did this kind of thing.

Or we were from the Netherlands.

WHEN EVERYTHING WAS SAID AND DONE, I HAD A BUNDLED-UP, NASTY, POOP-FILLED DIAPER IN ONE HAND AND AN ASSORTMENT OF POOPY SOCKS AND A POOPY PAIR OF JEANS IN THE OTHER.

Part of me wondered why we as a society didn't just allow toddlers to wander around outside with no pants on a normal basis. It would make things a lot easier.

I ended up wrapping up her little stinky bottom in my old gray Minnesota State hoodie, knotting it with the sleeves.

When everything was said and done, I had a bundled-up, nasty, poop-filled diaper in one hand and an assortment of poopy socks and a poopy pair of jeans in the other. Aspen still smelled horrible, and I'm sure I did too, but she didn't have nearly as much poop on her body. The hoodie around her waist looked like one of the wraps sumo wrestlers wear. She walked at first, but the hoodie kept coming loose, so I ended up carrying her most of the way.

By the time we got back to the van, I smelled like butthole, and so did Aspen, and Mel, and probably most of the corn maze. She was developing a rash along the back of her legs. I was getting a blister on the back of my foot from walking around with no socks, and the side of my shirt was spotted with toddler poop.

BY THE TIME WE GOT BACK TO THE VAN, I SMELLED LIKE BUTTHOLE, AND SO DID ASPEN, AND MEL, AND PROBABLY MOST OF THE CORN MAZE.

Aspen was moody and wiggly as I sat her down on the back of the van and changed her butt. I cleaned her off with wipes, the whole time feeling like a total idiot for not bringing the diaper bag.

I felt mostly sorry for Aspen. As I got her cleaned up, I told her I was sorry, and I promised I'd never forget the diaper bag again. But even then, I knew that forgetting the diaper bag wasn't the real problem.

I used almost a whole package of wipes. I put her in a new outfit. Then, instinctively, almost like an addiction, I reached into my pocket to check my phone. I started scrolling through Facebook, when Aspen reached out and wiped poop on my phone. Just a smudge the size of a pencil eraser.

But to be clear, I have an unwritten rule of no poop whatsoever on my phone, and although it wasn't much, it was by far the most poop I'd ever had on my phone, so I wasn't exactly happy about it.

I was so confident I'd cleaned up all the poop from the corn maze blowout, but obviously I hadn't. And as I looked at that small mustard-colored glob of toddler poop along the phone's screen, it seemed like a symbol, like Aspen was trying to tell me that I needed to give her my full attention so these sorts of things wouldn't happen.

Naturally, I'd used all the wipes, so I had to clean my phone on some dead grass next to the van. I didn't want to put it in my pocket because it surely still had poop germs on it, so I just set it in the back of the van.

I buckled Aspen into the car seat.

Then I sat in the front seat next to Mel, all the kids ready to head home, the whole van smelling like dust, corn, and poo. I turned over the motor, and Mel said in a snarky tone, "What? You aren't going to check your phone for ten minutes before we actually drive away, like usual?"

I didn't argue. I didn't take offense. I just said, "I put my phone in the back of the van, thank you very much."

Mel looked visibly shocked.

Then I looked in the rearview mirror. Aspen slightly nodded with approval from the back seat.

I'VE NEVER BEEN TO HELL, BUT I HAVE BEEN TO A LITTLE GIRL'S BIRTHDAY PARTY

I was in my backyard with several little girls between the ages of four and eight. I can't remember exactly how many were there, but it seemed like a lot. Far more than I recalled inviting. But when you have multiple kids at your house, it always feels like more than you expected, almost like kids under ten years old divide and multiply, similar to bacteria splitting when it comes into contact with other bacteria, crisscrossing their DNA, and eventually becoming something altogether new and dangerous.

It was a hot day in Oregon, close to 100°F (38°C), unusual weather for this part of the state. Norah was turning five, and this was her very special, first-time-having-friends-over, princess birthday bash.

I wanted it to be perfect. I wanted it to be an extraordinary party for a very wonderful little girl. I would never admit this publicly—well, outside of this book—but I longed to one-up the parties I'd seen online. I wanted something I could post about on social media, and all my friends would be jealous, and grudgingly like my posts, and I'd end up looking like a rock star dad.

Mel was not completely on board with this whole "show off to our Facebook friends" thing. But considering I hadn't ever been this involved in preparing one of our children's birthday parties, she went with the flow.

I pulled out all the stops.

Or at least, that's what I tried to do.

The princesses sat on a hodgepodge of folding chairs, dining room chairs, and sun-faded patio furniture that Mel covered with brightly colored bedsheets and then safety-pinned along the back, so they'd look like royal chairs. It was something she'd seen on Pinterest. I pulled our dining room table into the backyard and covered it with a princess-worthy tablecloth. In the center of the table were tea lights floating in a fishbowl. The Frozen soundtrack played in the background, and along the lattice attached to the patio hung some twinkling white Christmas lights.

We were under our porch awning. Even in the shade, it was intolerably hot. All the girls wore itchy, ill-fitting, Disney play dresses, one shoulder strap always falling down. It was an assortment of pastel pinks, blues, and purples, with plastic gold-framed pictures of princesses sewn over the hearts. Rapunzel, Snow White, Aurora, Ariel, Cinderella, Tiana, three Elsas, two Annas . . . everyone was accounted for.

Everyone wore tiaras.

The little redheaded sisters with snotty noses who lived two towns away wore tiaras.

The girl who lived up in the hills and didn't like to wash her hands wore a tiara.

The friends from school that talked too much wore tiaras.

The girls I didn't recognize wore tiaras.

Mel wore a tiara.

Strapped to Mel's chest was our new baby, Aspen, sleeping soundly and also wearing a tiara.

I wore a tiara.

But what really stood out was Norah, who was also wearing a tiara. But beneath it was a long blonde braided wig that dragged on the ground, just like in the movie *Tangled*. We found it online, and in the product picture, it looked a lot like Rapunzel's hair. But in real life, it made her look like my aunt who never grew out of her Dolly Parton phase and enjoys drinking vodka and ice water and often asks for a manager.

Norah didn't tell anyone she was Rapunzel, and I couldn't tell if she was disappointed with the wig or just unsure of herself while wearing it. But what I can say is that regardless of the heat, she refused to take it off, which was complicated considering the end of her braid was more or less a collection of leaves and dirt from our backyard.

THERE WERE TWO OPTIONS THAT WE COULD AFFORD: HAVE THE PARTY OUTSIDE, OR PUT DOWN A TARP IN THE LIVING ROOM. OUTSIDE SEEMED CLASSIER.

We decided to have the party outside weeks ago because little girls make huge messes, and a number of Norah's beautiful princess guests weren't 100 percent potty trained. Not that their parents didn't tell us they were, because they did. With earnest sincerity, they did. They came at us with total confidence in their child's ability to use the potty, but I'd found enough random wet spots on my furniture and had loaned enough of Norah's underwear to accident-prone girls over the summer to know that having them all in my house dressed as princesses, jacked up on cake and candy, was a surefire way to ruin my carpet.

There were two options that we could afford: have the party outside, or put down a tarp in the living room.

Outside seemed classier.

But two weeks before the party, the forecast

changed, and people were predicting this horrible heat wave. It killed our lawn and ruined our garden, and suddenly our backyard looked like Agrabah—which would have been fine if any of our guests were into Princess Jasmine, but unfortunately *Aladdin* was out of vogue and *Frozen* was very popular that year, leaving us in need of ice during a heat wave.

Mel and I were left to decide if we could hold the party outside or not.

"Will it ruin everything having it outside in 100 degrees?" I asked.

Mel shrugged.

Then we discussed how having the party inside would mean deep cleaning the house, and we didn't want to do that. I also felt like we'd get better pictures outside, but that was before the lawn died.

I thought a lot about how to get a nice picture to post online. Probably more than I should've, but honestly, no one keeps up with their neighbors anymore. I kept up with my Facebook friends.

It seemed like all of my friends were holding these parties in perfectly cleaned and organized houses, with stain-free carpet and walls painted one color and the trim another, with one wall that read "Blessed" in fancy cursive. These were parties with homemade cakes that were 2 feet tall and in the shape of Princess Aurora and worthy of a wedding reception, not to mention a piñata filled with custom gold candy coins that were stamped with a picture of the birthday girl.

I FELT LIKE I WAS IN THIS EMBARRASSING TUG-OF-WAR BETWEEN MAKING MY DAUGHTER'S FIFTH BIRTHDAY PARTY EXTRA, EXTRA SPECIAL—BECAUSE THAT'S WHAT I'D SEEN FROM OTHER PARENTS ONLINE—AND WHAT I COULD AFFORD, HAD THE SKILLS TO DO, AND HAD THE SANITY TO HANDLE.

These parties made me want to pull my eyes out of my head trying to figure out how the parents actually kept their house that clean while making an epic cake, while their children with perfectly braided hair and homemade gowns were all smiles and well behaved and . . . I could go on, but we were on a budget. I worked in education, and Mel was still finishing her degree. Our house was small and filled with clutter and kids that didn't give a crap. I felt like I was in this embarrassing tug-of-war between making my daughter's fifth birthday party extra, extra special—because that's what I'd seen from other parents online—and what I could afford, had the skills to do, and had the sanity to handle.

There was a lot of buildup to this party. Several arguments and a lot of excitement with some seriously high expectations for making everything wonderful.

In my mind, I saw it all as a royal event, where all the little girls complimented us on our party and walked around with royal dignity and grace, their pinkies pointed upward as they sipped tea. But once I was actually there, once it was all happening, it didn't feel like some social media-worthy royal extravaganza that all my friends would be jealous of.

Perhaps it was the heat, or the little girls screaming and fighting and laughing, or the sugar-high children with black, chocolate-covered teeth, or the lack of available cool drinking water, along with my dead garden, but it sure looked a lot like hell.

Was I being too dramatic?

Maybe.

IT SURE LOOKED A LOT LIKE HELL.

Or perhaps I was just struggling with the disappointment of not being able to replicate the awe-inspiring birthday parties I'd seen online.

The first game we played had similar rules to musical chairs, only the girls didn't get up while the music was going. Instead, Mel slowly walked around the circle of girls with a bottle of nail polish. I controlled the music, but I didn't really understand the game. I didn't understand why painting nails was such a big deal. I was second-guessing a lot of what we'd done for this party. I wanted Norah to feel special, but at the same time, I wondered if any of this was accomplishing our goal.

I stopped the music, and whoever was closest to Mel had a nail painted. The goal of the game was for one girl to have all her nails painted. She would be the winner. Only I didn't understand that. I thought the game stopped once everyone had at least one nail painted, which I will admit was a stupid assumption.

Who wants to paint only one nail?

I came to this conclusion because each time I stopped the music, every little girl that didn't have at least one painted nail flipped out. "This game isn't fair!" Or, "I never win anything!" An older girl even pointed her one painted finger across the patio and screamed, "I hate her!"

It felt like we invited Maleficent.

I'd never seen anything quite like this mix of rage and sorrow.

I started to time the music so each girl would have at least one painted nail because I am a fair and reasonable guy—and because it seemed like the best way to prevent a murder.

Eventually, Mel gave me a funny look, told me how the game was won, and asked why I was making it take so long. By then each girl had at least one nail painted, and as Mel and I spoke, several girls ran off into the yard, their arms in the air like fleeing prisoners, while the rest just sat there and gave one another the side-eye.

The whole party was like this—a struggle to keep the attention of these little girls so they wouldn't either run into the yard and pull plants out of the garden or run into the house and play with the bathroom sink. A friend of mine used to work at a drug and alcohol rehab clinic, and I couldn't help but think of some of the stories he'd told me of managing drug addicts as I watched Mel wrangle sunburning little girls in play dresses from the yard and back to the porch.

We were outnumbered, and the children knew it. Sometimes they split up, with one group running off into the yard while the other ran into the house. Sometimes they worked in a large group, crowding around the birthday cake and using their mighty numbers to overshadow their little fingers clawing at the frosting.

A FRIEND OF MINE USED TO WORK AT A DRUG AND ALCOHOL REHAB CLINIC, AND I COULDN'T HELP BUT THINK OF SOME OF THE STORIES HE'D TOLD ME OF MANAGING DRUG ADDICTS AS I WATCHED MEL WRANGLE SUNBURNING LITTLE GIRLS IN PLAY DRESSES FROM THE YARD AND BACK TO THE PORCH.

Eventually we gave up on the nail-painting game and moved on to opening presents.

The little girls sat in a circle on their royal chairs. Every gift was in pink and purple wrapping paper. All gifts were either Disney Princess–themed or soft and cuddly with big lovable eyes. With the opening of each gift, Norah held it over her head like it was a sacred relic. Every time, the girls responded with loud, terrifying screeching sounds that made the neighbor's dog bark.

Mel wandered around the party taking pictures with the legit-looking black camera she'd borrowed from her sister, Aspen strapped to her chest in a BabyBjörn, like some sort of a professional photographer taking a break from her maternity leave. I could see the frustration in her face. I can only imagine how difficult it was to get a good shot with these children screaming, their hair a mess, half their nails painted, the background as dry as the set of *Dune*.

After the presents, we served the cake. It was a midlevel buttercream sheet cake with princess figurines along the top, having what appeared to be a tea party. I had picked it up at the grocery store. It was supposed to say, "Have a Magical Birthday, Norah!" Only it didn't say much of anything anymore because the girls had been clawing at it, and the sun had melted it into a soupy mess.

Leading up to the party, I asked myself a lot of questions: I wondered if having a princess-themed party would exclude girls who couldn't afford a princess play dress and wondered if I should have some additional play dresses available. I wondered if people would judge the weeds in our lawn, and our sad, sagging back fence, and our garden that wasn't really a garden but a collection of dead cornstalks and a sad tomato plant. I asked if we needed to buy name-brand candy for the piñata, or if I could save a few bucks by filling it with off-brand 4 Musketeers and Ron's Peanut Butter Cups from the dollar store.

NEXT WAS THE PIÑATA. IT WAS SUPPOSED TO LOOK LIKE BELLE FROM *BEAUTY AND THE BEAST*. BUT TO ME IT JUST LOOKED LIKE A WOMAN IN A YELLOW DRESS HANGING FROM A ROPE.

And I absolutely asked myself if we should make our own cake or if buying a grocery store sheet cake would make us look like crappy parents. But the reality was that neither Mel nor I knew how to make a great cake, and we didn't have the money to pay for a professional cake, so this sheet cake with plastic figures seemed like a good middle ground.

Not that the children cared about any of that. They just shoved that cake into their grubby little mouths and then wiped the frosting along the front of their dresses, or the sheets on their chairs, or, in Norah's case, the wig.

Next was the piñata.

It was supposed to look like Belle from *Beauty and the Beast*. But to me it just looked like a woman in a yellow dress hanging from a rope. I know that we bought this piñata with the best of intentions, and while picking it out online I felt like it was going to be adorable. But once we went from theory to practice, the piñata took a disturbing twist. I slung the rope over the rafters, and reflected on the fact that I was hanging what looked like a woman from the patio and was about to ask little girls to beat her with a stick. The whole situation was morbid, but I didn't want to be a party pooper, so I just hung the stupid thing.

NOW WE HAD A HEADLESS PRINCESS HANGING IN OUR YARD WITH LITTLE GIRLS SCREAMING AND BEATING HER WITH A STICK.

We went from youngest to oldest. The first little girl was three or four years old. She approached the piñata nervously, not sure what she was going to do. But after the first swing, I could only describe the look in her eyes as bloodlust. She then started swinging with gusto, and eventually we had to pull her back and give another girl a try.

One of the older girls, who was probably seven, managed to knock off the princess's head, but the candy didn't come out, so I had to wrap a rope around her torso and string her up again. Now we had a headless princess hanging in our yard with little girls screaming and beating her with a stick. The whole event was not a shining moment for me as a father.

Eventually a little girl busted off the legs, spilling the piñata's insides. The children rushed at the candy, kicking the legless, headless princess to the side. The chocolate melted in the heat. The girls circled the princess's body. Their hands and faces were covered in melted chocolate that, from a distance, could have easily passed as blood.

It was terrifying.

But what was more frightening was when I looked at the clock.

The party was supposed to end at 4:00 p.m., but it was only 3:40 p.m. This meant that we'd run out of activities, and we still had a good twenty minutes before parents came to pick up their kids. And if these parents were anything like me, they'd be late.

Don't get me wrong, I love my kids. But I also savor the moments that I can spend alone with my wife, and being ten or fifteen minutes late to pick up the kids is excusable. I assume a lot of parents think this way. But usually, showing up late to pick up your kids means leaving the caregiver with just one or two extra kids. Not a bazillion little girls full of bloodlust and chocolate. Long story short, I knew that it would be 30 to 45 minutes before I got all these "princesses" out of my yard, and we had no more activities in our back pockets.

I looked at Mel. "What are we going to do?"

Mel looked at me with fear in her eyes. "I. Don't. Know. . . ."

BASICALLY, I CLOSED MY EYES AND PRAYED FOR THE BEST. IT WASN'T UNTIL LATER THAT I REALIZED THE LITTLE TERRORS HAD PULLED UP OUR TOMATO PLANT AND PLACED A BARBIE HEAD ON A POPSICLE® STICK NEXT TO THE BIRDBATH, IN WHAT I ASSUMED WAS SOME *LORD OF THE FLIES* EXPRESSION OF DOMINANCE.

I thought about letting them finish coloring the pictures they started at the beginning of the party but soon noticed all the crayons had melted in the sun. The girls started wandering into the house, which I didn't want, so we let them into the yard and hoped that they didn't destroy our already dying grass.

Basically, I closed my eyes and prayed for the best. It wasn't until later that I realized the little terrors had pulled up our tomato plant and placed a Barbie head on a Popsicle® stick next to the birdbath, in what I assumed was some *Lord of the Flies* expression of dominance.

Thinking back, I probably should've just started

a game of tag or red light–green light, but by this point I was tired, dehydrated, and frustrated because nothing had gone according to plan.

I wasn't thinking at my regular capacity.

Eventually, parents arrived. Many of them late, like I suspected.

Once the party was over, I started cleaning up. In my yard, I found candy wrappers, chewed gum, melted chocolate, cake frosting, a new colony of ants, the piñata torso, a scabby Disney Princess BAND-AID®, a high-heeled plastic princess dress shoe, popped balloons, melted candles, four tiaras, three princess goody bags, two boogers, and one piñata head.

I didn't find my dignity, but I did find some disappointment.

Once I got things cleaned up, I plopped down in the living room's easy chair. Norah was playing with one of her new toys, still wearing her soiled wig and her play dress that was now spackled with frosting and crayon.

She climbed into my lap to show me her new toy, a big-eyed, tie-dyed stuffed animal of some sort.

I thought about my high hopes. I thought about how I intended to share all of it online but didn't end up with even one decent picture.

"That's cute," I said. "Did you have fun at your party?"

Norah looked at me with a big smile and nodded excitedly. She rambled on for some time, talking about her friends, and her gifts, and all the candy she ate.

"You weren't disappointed?" I asked.

She looked at me like I was crazy, like she'd just had the time of her life.

Then she asked if she could have another party tomorrow.

With five-year-olds, everything is tomorrow.

The look in her eyes made me realize this party was the highlight of her life thus far.

And suddenly all the buildup, all those feelings of keeping up with our online friends, all that disappointment didn't matter anymore.

Leave it to my five-year-old to put things into perspective.

"Good," I said. "I'm glad you enjoyed yourself."

She snuggled into my chest, and we sat there for a while, both of us smelling like frosting.

REASONS MY CHILDREN HAVE CRIED AT THEIR OWN BIRTHDAY PARTIES

My children have cried a lot at their own birthday parties. Way more than I expected, despite someone once writing a song about this sort of thing. Naturally, it's gotten a little better with age, but not really. And there have been a number of times that I was the source of the tears. Not intentionally, mind you. I didn't get up in the morning and say, "I'm going to make my kid cry at their party." I'm not a *Scooby-Doo* villain. I know that for a fact, because I don't own a haunted amusement park and I haven't worn a mask since 2007, when I dressed up as Nacho Libre for Halloween.

I need to stop defending myself here. Just read on. I'll let you decide if I was being a jerk.

I sang "Happy Birthday."

When Norah turned two, we sang her "Happy Birthday" like any good parents should. However, apparently she didn't want me to sing. She was okay with Mom singing, and Grandma singing, and Aunt Lucinda singing, and Tristan singing (although he refused to). But she specifically asked that I not sing. Why? Because two-year-olds are finicky enigmas with sticky hands, and as much as I understood that, I got a little offended. I have a nice voice, right? I wanted to sing "Happy Birthday" to my very sweet little birthday girl. Is that really too much to ask? So rather than take no for an answer, when everyone started singing, I just stood behind her high chair and sang too. Then, right before the last "happy birthday to you" I jumped out from behind the chair to let her know I'd been singing the whole time. I assumed she'd realize that it was okay for me to sing, and that I was actually a very good singer, and that there was nothing dangerous about her father singing. Instead she cried for an hour, never blew out her candles, and my own mother said, "You just couldn't keep your mouth shut, could you?"

I wouldn't buy a hoverboard.

When my son was ten, his best friend got a hoverboard. Tristan asked that we get him one for his birthday. Now, when he said his friend got a hoverboard, I immediately thought of that scene in *Back to the Future II* where McFly outruns the bully on a flying skateboard, and for the first time in a very long time I imagined myself as Michael J. Fox. But once I found out that this was not a wheel-less, gravity-defying skateboard but a miniature Segway without a handle, I decided against it. Why? Well, I don't want to say that he was a full-blown slug of a boy, but getting Tristan out of the house to use his actual legs usually took a bribe of some kind—or allowing him to play *Pokémon GO*. It was all very frustrating, so the last thing I was going to give him was a lithium-powered source of transportation that he could use to catch Pokémon. Where I went wrong was when he suggested the idea, I got visibly excited thinking it was an actual hoverboard in the futuristic sense. I even exclaimed, "What? They have hoverboards now? Dude! I want one!" He assumed my excitement was a lock. Then, when he got a pretty sweet SpongeBob skateboard on his birthday, he complained and I told him the simple truth that I wouldn't get him any source of transportation unless he was the motor. So he cried a little. I told him I was sorry. We shared a hug. But I still didn't buy him a hoverboard.

I burned the cupcakes.
Each half-birthday, Mel makes the kids cupcakes and tells them how special they are, and naturally the kids love it. I could take or leave this tradition.

However, I will admit, I never turn down cupcakes on my half-birthday because, as stated on page 139, I'm not a *Scooby-Doo* villain. Anyway, Mel was at a women's conference during Aspen's half-birthday. She was four and a half, and I don't know who told her it was her half-birthday, because she couldn't read a calendar. Full confession: I wasn't completely sure it was her half-birthday, because I'd forgotten the exact date of her birthday. I thought about texting Mel for a reminder, but considering I had to call her for birthday information every time I filled out a medical form for my children, I decided it would be easier to just make it her half-birthday. Aspen demanded cupcakes until I was ready to sit in the garage with the car running and go into that deep sleep. So I made cupcakes, something I obviously suck at, because I burned them and set off the fire alarm, which was super loud, and all the kids cried until I finally ordered pizza.

I threw away the box.
We got Norah this big kitchen play set for her fifth birthday, and when I was done building it, I threw away the box. I suppose I should have known better. She was having a great time inside the box as I put together the play set, but it was taking up half the living room. So while she was in the tub washing all the cake frosting from her little face, I cut up the box and put it in the recycling. I assumed she'd be more excited to play with the

toy I got her than the box it came in. But that was stupid, and she was inconsolable well into the night, not interested in the toy she begged us for but rather the box. In her defense, I did have many a good time with a cardboard box as a child, so I understood. I once used a bunch of my mom's Diet Coke boxes to turn myself into a Transformer, and I still list that accomplishment on my resume. I eventually apologized by giving her an extra piece of cake that, I'd like to add, did stop her from crying but also sent her over the edge with a full-blown birthday sugar rush, and I didn't get to bed until after midnight. When she crashed, it was in my arms, and both of us slept on the couch well into the night. It was pretty sweet until she woke up in the morning and remembered the box and started crying again.

I don't think I ever did anything wrong, per se, when my children cried on their birthdays. But I didn't exactly do all the things right either. These moments fell into a middle ground between right and wrong, where things could have gone better, but none of it was done maliciously. I'm not exactly sure what to call that place between right and wrong. I'm don't know if it has an official name, but for the sake of this book I'm just going to call it parenting.

THE DAY WE CAUGHT OUR KIDS LOOKING AT THEIR BUTTHOLES

It was a Friday night—Mel's birthday, actually. I'd just placed candles in the cake and was washing my hands at the sink when Mel approached me in faded blue jeans and a pink shirt, her arms folded, and softly said, "I walked in on our kids looking at their buttholes."

It took me longer than I'd like to admit to figure out exactly what she'd said. I mean, yes, she clearly pronounced the words. She spoke in a complete sentence that I comprehended, but the part of my brain where one synapse connects with the other seemed unable to interpret this information, and frankly, I felt a little dizzy. I was able to force it all through my brain, however, and found myself left with a question that I, as a father, never fathomed: Why were my children looking at their buttholes?

I played a scene out in my head in which a naked six-year-old Tristan and four-year-old Norah bent over and giggled, one eye closed, something similar to when a pirate looks through a telescope. It seemed innocent enough. But the more I thought about it, the stranger it became.

Moments earlier, I had been getting the kids ready for bed.

SOMEHOW IN THE FEW MOMENTS IT TOOK ME TO WALK DOWN THE HALL TO THE KITCHEN TO PUT CANDLES ON MEL'S CAKE, OUR CHILDREN HAD WANDERED INTO THE SAME ROOM AND DECIDED TO EXPLORE THEIR BUTTHOLES.

I'd started filling both our bathtubs. Then I stepped into the kitchen while Tristan and Norah got undressed, separately, in their own rooms. Somehow in the few moments it took me to walk down the hall to the kitchen to put candles on Mel's cake, our children had wandered into the same room and decided to explore their buttholes.

I tried to tell myself that it was probably nothing, but at the same time I was old enough to know that little things can sometimes lead to big things. For example: A boy I grew up with used to snort Pixy Stix®. Now don't get me wrong, it was fun to watch. We all had a good laugh. But I will admit that nothing about his shooting flavored sugar up his nose sat right with me. I never trusted him. Twenty years later, he was the target of a full-blown O. J. Simpson–style car chase over meth, which is terrible considering his childhood aspiration was to become an astronaut.

Was my son going to grow up and become that dude in Central Park in nothing but a trench coat and black socks flashing strangers? Would I someday get an email informing me that my daughter appeared on a *Girls Gone Wild* sort of program, showing strangers (the world) her butthole?

Mel and I stood in the kitchen.

"Hold on," I said. "Say that again."

WAS MY SON GOING TO GROW UP AND BECOME THAT DUDE IN CENTRAL PARK IN NOTHING BUT A TRENCH COAT AND BLACK SOCKS FLASHING STRANGERS? WOULD I SOMEDAY GET AN EMAIL INFORMING ME THAT MY DAUGHTER APPEARED ON A *GIRLS GONE WILD* SORT OF PROGRAM, SHOWING STRANGERS (THE WORLD) HER BUTTHOLE?

Mel gave me a look that seemed to say, "I'm as confused as you." Then she scratched the back of her head and told the story again, slower this time.

"I was in Norah's room when I overheard her say in the bathroom, 'What's that hole in your butt?'

Then Tristan said, 'It's my butthole. Want to look at it?' I heard laughter. Once I came into the bathroom, things had obviously progressed because Tristan was now looking at Norah's butthole."

"Did you say anything to them?" I asked, hopeful that perhaps she'd already dealt with it and I was in the clear. Maybe she was just letting me know it happened, so I could help keep an eye out for further butthole exploration, hopeful that there would never, ever be another butthole problem.

She didn't say she broke it up or had a talk about appropriate butthole behavior. She just looked me in the eyes and said, "It's my birthday."

She was pulling the birthday card.

I couldn't blame her. Were it my birthday, the last thing I'd want to do was spend it chatting with our children about looking at each other's buttholes.

"Oh crap," I said. "Okay. How exactly do you suggest I handle this?"

I didn't say it with confrontation, or anger, or anything close to it.

I said it with desperation, and confusion, and . . . a little fear. Part of me was hopeful that it would go away on its own, but the mature adult in me knew that it might not, and I needed to do something PDQ.

I never looked at my siblings' buttholes, so I was at a loss as to what to do. I thought about asking Mel if she ever examined any of her family's buttholes. Perhaps this was a normal thing with a standardized text parents have been using for decades, kind of like how people say, "We talked about the birds and the bees." Maybe there was a siblings-looking-at-their-buttholes equivalent: We talked about the curious rabbit and the dried apricot.

My mind was wandering pretty quickly. I was panicking. I'll admit it. For a hot moment I thought about asking Mel if she ever looked at her siblings' buttholes, but I quickly realized I didn't want to know, so I didn't ask her any of those questions and just assumed I'd be tackling this without a script.

I WAS PANICKING. I'LL ADMIT IT. FOR A HOT MOMENT I THOUGHT ABOUT ASKING MEL IF SHE EVER LOOKED AT HER SIBLINGS' BUTTHOLES . . .

I assumed Tristan and Norah were too young for this to be a sexual thing. Or at least I hoped so. I wasn't ready for any of that. But it did feel like we were moving into some strange new territory as parents, a land where brothers and sisters freely looked at each other's buttholes.

A place I'd rather my children not be.

But I suppose thinking too much about my children's childhood actions and how they might damage their future was a huge part of my panic. All of it gave me a horrible feeling that I needed to get this thing right, but what did that even mean? I doubted I'd ever gotten anything totally right as a father, and considering I was going to chat with my children about looking at their buttholes, the possibility of success was really low.

I thought about how my parents would have handled a situation like this. They were boomers, and I have a strong feeling my mother would have asked my father to handle it too. Only he would have done nothing and then lied to my mother about handling it, the whole time assuming it would just go away. In contrast, I was a millennial father, a more hands-on, compassionate breed that spoke with my children about anything and would help them through any problem they faced. But the millennial-father handbook didn't mention anything about buttholes, and all of this made me wish we were raising our children in the '80s.

I THOUGHT ABOUT HOW MY PARENTS WOULD HAVE HANDLED A SITUATION LIKE THIS. THEY WERE BOOMERS, AND I HAVE A STRONG FEELING MY MOTHER WOULD HAVE ASKED MY FATHER TO HANDLE IT . . .

"Just go tell them that it's not appropriate and that they shouldn't do it anymore," Mel said in a matter-of-fact tone.

She made it sound so simple.

I knew I needed to chat with them tonight, or they'd forget about the whole thing. Young kids are like that. I considered chatting with them that evening, as we all sat at the table eating birthday cake. But then I imagined a moment after Mel blew out her candles but before we finished eating cake when I leaned forward, looked my kids in the eyes, and said, "Stop looking at your buttholes."

Pretty sure that would ruin Mel's birthday, so I decided to talk to them individually as they bathed.

I approached Norah first.

She was stretched out in the tub, her head half underwater.

NORAH WAS AT THAT AGE WHERE SHE SAID OKAY TO JUST ABOUT ANYTHING SHE WAS CONFRONTED WITH AND THEN ALMOST IMMEDIATELY FORGOT WHAT SHE AGREED TO.

I asked if she'd looked at Tristan's butthole. She didn't giggle. She didn't get offended, or angry, or anything like that. She just cried out in her chipper, four-year-old voice, "Yup!"

I had to step from the room to keep from laughing. I stood in the hallway for a while, my back against the wall. She started to giggle.

Once I came back, I told Norah to never look at her brother's butthole again.

"Okay," she said. "I won't ever, ever, ever,

ever . . . look at Tristan's butthole ever again."

Norah was at that age where she said okay to just about anything she was confronted with and then almost immediately forgot what she agreed to.

I wasn't as worried about her because she was so young. I was more worried about Tristan, who was a little older and much more argumentative.

As I walked to our master bathroom, I ran a few heartfelt parenting speeches through my head. All of them seemed to start with, "When a young boy becomes a man," or, "Curiosity is normal," but nothing I could think of fit the subject matter.

Once I got to my son, all of those long-winded, *Leave It to Beaver*, life-changing dad speeches went out the window and I simply said, "Dude! Don't look at your sister's butthole."

He was naked, sprawled out in the tub, water up to his chest, his mouth in a partial frown, hands at his sides.

He started laughing.

Tristan was a complex little guy. When faced with a situation he didn't like or didn't understand, he laughed. I did the same thing when I was young, so I understood his logic. But what I didn't understand as a boy was how infuriating it is to try to talk to someone about a serious subject and have the person laugh in your face.

"Stop laughing," I said. "This is serious. You can't do that. Do you ever see Mom and I looking at our buttholes?"

The moment that came out of my mouth, I knew it was the wrong thing to say.

Tristan thought for a moment. Then he laughed and said, "No. But it'd be really funny if you did."

I stood silently for a moment.

Rather than linger on what was obviously a bad comparison, I kept talking. Or maybe a better word is "rambling." Something came over me. I dove into my fears. I mentioned how I loved him, and how the last thing I wanted was for him to grow up with a loose understanding of decency. I didn't want him wandering about, obsessed with buttholes, or showing random people his butthole. I told him that he should never put his butthole online and how important it is to keep your butthole covered. I can't recall everything I said, but I know I went on for a while, finally concluding with, "You'll never become an astronaut by showing people your butthole."

Tristan had this look that wasn't exactly fear, but it wasn't exactly comprehension either. It seemed to fall somewhere between, "This is my father so I need to listen," and, "My father is insane."

"I won't look at Norah's butthole anymore!" he said. "Gosh!"

Later that night, we were all at the table eating birthday cake. Tristan was in blue two-piece *Skylanders* pajamas, his brown hair messy and dark with bathwater. Norah was in pink and yellow zip-up footed pajamas with a flower print, her short brown hair wet and freshly combed down the middle. We'd already sung "Happy Birthday." The candles trailed with smoke.

Tristan broke the silence, speaking through a mouth full of chocolate cake, "Dad told me I'd never be an astronaut if I kept looking at Norah's butthole."

Mel looked at me, then at Tristan, and then at me again. Her head shook slightly, and it seemed like it was her turn to struggle with comprehending a situation. Then she mouthed, "Really?"

"DAD TOLD ME I'D NEVER BE AN ASTRONAUT IF I KEPT LOOKING AT NORAH'S BUTTHOLE."

I shrugged.

And then she said something that I'd heard from her countless times before, but I don't know if it'd never made my face this red: "Don't you think you overreacted?"

I don't know why my mind jumps from one thing to another and then to another, and suddenly I'm fearful that some innocent action will push my children out of NASA and into prison. But what I do know is that as Mel looked at me, I fully realized that I probably had overreacted.

Mel reached across the table and took Tristan's

hand and said, "Buttholes have nothing to do with astronauts." Which I'd like to say isn't exactly correct. Astronauts have buttholes. Every single one of them. But what she said next I couldn't argue with. She looked our son in the eyes and said, "What your father was trying to tell you is that looking at your sister's butthole is inappropriate. You are going to grow up to do really great things, but you will need to respect other people's bodies along the way."

This was the most oddly maternal thing I'd ever heard, but considering the situation, it was perfect.

Tristan looked at his mother. He didn't laugh and he didn't argue with her. He simply wrapped his pinky around his mother's, his face stern like he was about to sign a contract, a little chocolate frosting still on his hand, and said, "Pinkie swear."

MY SON PAID OFF HIS DEBT WITH BIRTHDAY MONEY. I'D NEVER BEEN PROUDER. HE'D NEVER BEEN MORE DISAPPOINTED.

A few months before Tristan's 12th birthday, he asked to borrow money to download the new release of *Legend of Zelda* on our Nintendo, and we offered him a loan instead.

Why?

Because he sucked with money.

It was a fact.

He was the burn-a-hole-in-your-pocket kind of kid. He was the I'll-pay-you-back kid, the I-promise-I-will kid, the you-can-trust-me kid. When he asked to borrow money for that game, he already owed me money, along with his grandma, sister, mother, the Mob, Deutsche Bank. . . . To be honest, if Lucifer popped up from under Tristan's bed and asked if he wanted to use his soul as collateral to get a down payment on a specialty pack of *Pokémon* cards, the kid would have taken the deal. Perhaps this had already happened—I was having a hard time keeping track of all his debts, and frankly, so was he.

HE WAS LIKE LIVING WITH A SHADY COUSIN WHO HAD A BIG-TIME BUSINESS PLAN BUT JUST NEEDED A FEW BUCKS TO GET OFF THE GROUND.

Tristan never asked to borrow a huge amount of money, only a few bucks here and there. Usually to download a game or buy some candy. If we added up all his debts, he was probably in the hole $40. But at eleven years old, $40 is a significant amount of money.

And frankly, it was getting old. He was like living with a shady cousin who had a big-time business plan but just needed a few bucks to get off the ground. It was a growing problem, and by the time he asked to borrow money for that Nintendo game, I'd started to imagine him as an adult, and it looked a lot like Johnny Boy (Robert De Niro) in *Mean Streets*, owing everyone money and everyone wanting to punch him in the face for it.

Or worse.

So instead of just handing over the cash like usual, we found a family loan agreement online. We made a payment plan, added a percentage, and consequences for missed or late payments. We even broke down how much more he'd be paying with interest in a spreadsheet. We wanted this to be as real as possible, hopeful that he'd learn to manage his money better and stop taking out loan after loan, digging himself further into debt.

And it's probably best to come clean here. I suggested the loan, sure. But Mel, she did the calculations. She's the real money manager in the family.

I studied English.

Before marriage, I wasn't exactly horrible with my money. But I wasn't awesome either. My late teens and early twenties were a long list of credit cards and overdraft fees. There was the time I ran out of money and couldn't make rent and had to move back in with my mother. I was 21. There was the time I put a pro-level mountain bike on a credit card and was almost sent to collections because of missed payments. There was the money my grandmother gave me for college, and I blew it on, well, burgers and fries.

By the time I met Mel, I'd gotten better. When we got married, I showed her a shoebox full of cash in different envelopes with rent, car payment, fun money, and a number of other bills written on them. I winked and said, "See? I know how to manage my money."

This envelope system was a step up, sure, but Mel looked at my shoebox full of cash, and then looked at me like I couldn't tie my shoes.

"Have you heard of Excel?" she asked.

It was then that she started managing our money.

We showed the spreadsheet to Tristan at the kitchen table, and his eyes glossed over. It was pretty clear that he didn't care about any of that, only the game, and all I could think about was the first time I signed a car loan. The interest was somewhere in the teens, and I recall saying to myself, "Fourteen isn't that big of a number. . . ."

THIS ENVELOPE SYSTEM WAS A STEP UP, SURE, BUT MEL LOOKED AT MY SHOEBOX FULL OF CASH, AND THEN LOOKED AT ME LIKE I COULDN'T TIE MY SHOES.

I told Tristan that the payment would be close to 50 percent of his "income." He was given a small allowance for sweeping and mopping the floors each week, cleaning out the van, and keeping up with his homework.

"It's never a good decision to take out a loan with payments that high," I said.

He looked me dead in the eyes, almost like he was about to heed my warning, and then shrugged, happily signed, and downloaded the game.

Two months in, it happened. He didn't do all of his chores over the month, and he bought another game and some candy, so he missed a payment.

We held a "financial meeting" in the kitchen. Mel and I sat on one side of our black dining room table. Tristan sat on the other, his hair mashed on one side from sleep, his blue charter school hoodie spackled with crumbs. He wasn't exactly dressed to impress, but at that age, he never was.

THEN HE SAID—BRACE YOURSELF— "WHAT'RE YOU GOING TO DO ABOUT IT?"

Our gray family MacBook was open with the payment information, and the printed and signed contract was between us on the table. We asked him about his missing payment, and he gave us a shrug.

Then he said—brace yourself—"What're you going to do about it? I already passed the game."

It was then that Mel leaned forward and read the second paragraph of the loan, the one where he put his game systems up as collateral. They would now be repossessed until he was back in good standing (which meant the minimum payment plus a $6 late charge).

I half-smiled, looked at my wife, and winked. *Gotcha*, I thought.

But had we?

I assumed this would be a huge lightbulb moment for Tristan. He'd look us both in the face and say, "Thank you for this lesson. I will now go forth and only borrow money reasonably. When I make my millions, I will be sure to put you two in a quality rest home, *not* something affordable that has been featured on *Dateline*."

He might even hug me.

But he didn't do anything like that.

At first his eyes got misty, like he was going to cry. Then he let out a deep breath, his face red, fists at his sides, and ran into his room and slammed the door.

He went through a number of emotions in just a few hours.

Disbelief: "How can you do this to me?"

Desperation: "How much can I earn by picking up after the dog?"

Boredom: "I'm sooooo bored." (Times infinity.)

Quiet disdain: He glared at Mel and me for a considerable amount of time, hopeful that we would crack under the shame of his eyes.

And naturally, I was left to wonder if we'd made the right decision.

At the moment, I just didn't know. During those first few days, I was confident that I'd failed him and I'll tell you why.

Years earlier, when I lived in Minnesota, I was chatting with a buddy of mine who worked as a financial adviser. He was going on about how he was great at giving advice but horrible with his own money. I was helping him move into a new house. I asked him why he thought he was so bad with his money, and he told me that his father used to comment on the things he'd buy. He called them stupid and pointless, and it only caused him to hide all of his purchases and in turn spend money secretly. Three months later, the bank foreclosed on that house, and his wife divorced him.

I couldn't help but think about that moment and compare it to how Tristan was reacting to us taking his video games away. Was this entire thing going to backfire, and suddenly Tristan was going to go in the wrong direction and take out all the loans? I didn't know. But one thing was pretty clear: He hated me, and I wondered if he would hate me forever.

And it's not like I had any right to be cocky. I didn't understand how money worked until the first time I got a late charge on my rent, or until I was two clicks from getting my truck repossessed, or until I spent almost ten grand on a credit card and then had to struggle for several years to pay it back. I was trying to give my son a little taste of all that now rather than later.

But who loves the loan officer or the repo man? No one!

And Mel and I were now both.

Tristan stopped talking to me for a few days outside of asking for food. Mostly he communicated via grunts and long, agonizing sighs.

Every day, I thought about giving in so he'd talk to me again.

But we stuck to the terms of the loan. We dug in our heels and hoped for the best, because as much as it sucked for all of us, I wished someone would've done something like this for me when I was young.

Six months after the loan, and three months after taking away all the game systems, Tristan and I were browsing at a video game store.

We were talking again, but he was sulking between the aisles. It was the day before his birthday, and he was trying to figure out what he wanted.

I could see it in his eyes. He wasn't looking forward to his birthday because everything he wanted needed a game system. He didn't blame his own poor money choices, and he didn't blame the loan. I don't think he even blamed his mother, because those two were pretty tight. He blamed me. I could feel it, and I was just waiting for him to say that I ruined his 12th birthday.

I was looking at some stuffed *Mario Bros.* figures, waiting for him to make a decision, when he walked up to my side and tugged at my shirt.

"How much birthday money do I have?" he asked.

I added up how much Mel and I had set aside for his birthday gift with how much his grandparents had sent him. I gave him a total.

He thought for a moment, calculated a few things in his head, and said, "I could get out of debt with that and still have $10."

"Yeah," I said. "You could."

We went back and forth for a bit. He negotiated a payoff number that left him with $15 instead of $10 for his birthday. I couldn't help but be proud of him for that.

He looked at the ground. He kicked the store carpet with his shoe. And then he said, "I'm going to pay off my debt so I can have my systems back."

He said it like he'd totaled his car right before a huge senior road trip, or he'd been dumped before prom, or he'd been cut from the team right before the big game, or any other number of huge letdowns he might face in the next few years.

"But now my birthday is going to suck," he said.

And while I was pretty sure he still didn't like me, and it was obvious that this whole loan thing had ruined his 12th birthday, I couldn't stop smiling at him.

"Stop it," he said.

"I can't."

"Why not?"

"Because I'm proud of you."

EVERYDAY FAILS

I HANDLED MY DAUGHTER'S FIRST CRUSH HORRIBLY

Mel laughed as she told me about some little creep kissing my daughter at church. He was five years old. It was during Sunday school. I would've hoped that kissing my daughter while at a church would get this boy struck down, but apparently God doesn't work that way, and suddenly I was left feeling cheated both as a father and a Christian. I mean, come on! I wasn't expecting a Sodom and Gomorrah kind of air strike. I didn't want the boy turned into a pillar of salt or anything, but I at least expected a temporary paralysis. Or for the boy to go blind for a time. Or perhaps to be swallowed by a whale.

I paid tithing.

I read my scriptures.

I was a good follower of God.

Wasn't I entitled to retribution?

What a joke.

According to Mel, after the children sang "I Am a Child of God," she noticed that Norah was holding Jonathon's hand. Then he leaned over and kissed her on the cheek.

"It was absolutely adorable!" she exclaimed, leaning up and onto her toes. "They're so cute together!"

I DIDN'T WANT THE BOY TURNED INTO A PILLAR OF SALT OR ANYTHING, BUT I AT LEAST EXPECTED A TEMPORARY PARALYSIS.

Norah was four, and frankly, I was head over heels for that little girl. Sometimes I asked her if she'd stay cute and little and love me forever. She always said yes in this adorable, high-pitched little voice. Then, with a hand on one hip, she gave me this look that seemed to say, "Of course I'm going to love you forever." But I knew it wasn't true. Someday I'd cramp her style. Someday I'd become an embarrassment. Someday she'd fall in love and leave me, probably much sooner than I'd like, and the thought of that broke my heart.

I felt a white-hot heat in my stomach as Mel told me about some boy kissing my little Norah. I wanted to approach this boy and tell him personally to keep his grubby, sticky, gropey, booger-coated hands off my daughter. I found nothing about this situation cute, or funny, or adorable. I went cold. I felt anxious. I kind of wanted to fight this kid. However, I knew that wasn't the best route, considering he was a little boy, and I was a grown man, and beating him up was a great way to make trending news and/or go to prison.

I asked a lot of questions. I asked what Norah's response was. I asked if he asked her before he did it. I asked if he touched her inappropriately, or if she touched him inappropriately. I asked if he had any plans for the future. I asked if he was going to go to college, or trade school, or if he had any real ambition, or if he was just going to keep living in his parents' house.

I asked if he had a criminal record.

Actually, I didn't ask *all* of those questions. But I thought about asking them. I wanted to ask them, but when I discussed his college plans Mel cut me off with, "It was just a cute innocent thing between two kids."

So I dropped it.

But I wasn't buying it.

Naturally, I knew Jonathon. He was this confident kid with a random sense of humor and a passion for wearing video game costumes to social functions. I even kind of liked the kid before he started getting all smoochy with my daughter. I knew his parents. They were good people. His father was a PhD candidate. His mother was kind and soft-spoken. They were an all-around good, hardworking family.

And when I stacked all the things up, it did seem like he was a pretty good churchgoing kid who might happen to be into cosplay, but I couldn't necessarily hold that against him because it's now socially acceptable for some reason.

But the problem obviously wasn't the boy—it was me. Why on earth was I thinking this way four years into raising my daughter? I couldn't believe how one little kiss at church could cause me to go down these different paths, everything from considering if this young boy had aspirations, to wanting to fight the kid, to hoping God would feed him to a whale. Neither of them had enrolled in kindergarten yet.

Sure, Norah was my first daughter, and when I found out I was going to have a daughter, I thought about a lot of things. I thought about how confusing it might be. I thought about how there would be a learning curve. But I never considered I'd fall into that protective dad cliché.

Not long before the kiss, we were at Jonathon's home playing board games. I should have known something was up between them that night.

The adults were playing Monopoly in the kitchen. I went to check on the kids in the living room, to find Jonathon singing as Norah sat on a small wooden chair and watched. She clapped every so often and swooned a little, her small butt wiggling in the chair to the sound of Jonathon's voice. Jonathon was dressed as Mario, in blue corduroy overalls fastened with yellow buttons and a red long-sleeve shirt and poofy red hat. On his lip was a false mustache, and although I love Mario, you just can't trust someone with a mustache. I'm sorry.

Furthermore, video game costumes were this kid's thing. On Sundays, his parents obviously fought him into a shirt and tie, but every other day of the week, Jonathon was Link, or Luigi, or Ash. He seemed to have an endless assortment of video game costumes and never really dressed as himself, making me wonder who he really was.

LONG STORY SHORT, DRESSING UP AS MARIO WAS NOT THE WARDROBE I'D HAVE PICKED WHEN IMPRESSING A GIRL, BUT I SUPPOSE I DON'T HAVE A LOT OF ROOM TO JUDGE. I WORE JNCO JEANS AND BLEACHED THE TIPS OF MY HAIR IN THE '90S.

And you know, at his young age, dressing up every day as a character from a video game was forgivable. But mark my words, if twenty-something Norah brought home some dude dressed as Mario for dinner, and it wasn't Halloween or a comic con, I'd side-eye the heck out of that guy. I'd ask questions. I might even suggest an intervention or a stint in a psych ward.

Long story short, dressing up as Mario was not the wardrobe I'd have picked when impressing a girl, but I suppose I don't have a lot of room to judge. I wore JNCO jeans and bleached the tips of my hair in the '90s. Let's just say I did it all for the nookie. Although I managed all of my own nookie.

This Mario costume did seem to be working for Jonathon, though. Norah was obviously twitterpated by this kid. In his hand was a long yellow dart with a red suction cup on one end. He used it as a microphone, his hips swinging, right heel pounding out a beat. He kept singing, "I choose you. You. You."

With each "you," Norah put her hand over her mouth or her heart and giggled or smiled longingly—the same smile she often gave me when I came home from work. I laughed for some time. I didn't really think anything was up, and you know what, there wasn't. I don't think they had any idea what they were doing outside of having a good time. But when I reflect back on my life, some of the worst decisions I've ever made revolved around a good time.

A few hours after Mel told me about Norah's kiss, I sat down next to Norah on our faded gray love seat. We were living in this crappy three-bedroom, third-floor apartment. Norah's hands were curled down like paws, and she was sniffing the armrest and wiggling her bottom like a puppy.

Pretending to be a puppy was her new thing. She was all about running around the house on all fours, barking when someone knocked on the door and drinking water by shoving her face in a bowl. I'm not going to say I understood the appeal of pretending to be a puppy, but what I can say is that it was getting pretty difficult to get Norah to speak in anything outside of dog.

"Tell me about Jonathon," I said.

"Ruff, ruff," she replied.

"Norah," I said. "I want to know what happened."

Norah sat up, crawled into my lap, and licked my arm. Then she began speaking in the third person, like she often did when pretending to be a dog.

"Ringo wants to play fetch."

I told her that kisses are very special things and that she needed to save them for very special people. Like her mother and her father. "You only should be kissing people you really love. Not just any old boy dressed like a plumber."

She got quiet for a moment, just long enough for me to think that I was getting through to her. Then she looked up at me, smiled, and said, "Ringo farted on your leg."

I wasn't getting anywhere. So I tried a different strategy. I told her that there was something in her mouth. She furrowed her brow, her face a mix of fear and confusion. Her paws straightened out, and she looked up at me.

"What is it?" she asked.

"I'm not sure. Open wider."

She opened her mouth and I let out a confused "hmmmm."

I told her it was a boy monster. She looked scared as I looked closer.

"Yup," I said. "Definitely a boy monster. The crazy thing about boy monsters is that you can't feel them. You don't even know they're there. But they scare boys away."

It's not too often that I feel this clever. I recall thinking that this was probably the best idea I'd ever had.

I told her that boy monsters are the most wonderful things in the world, better than slap bracelets (an accessory that had recently experienced a renaissance among children her age).

"You really are very lucky to have a boy monster," I said.

"Take it out," Norah said.

"Can't," I said. I searched my mind for a responsible age. An age that I felt was old enough. Mature enough. An age at which I could say, "Yeah. Norah's ready to date."

"It has to stay in there until you are twenty-eight years old."

This was only three years younger than I was at the time. It was also six years older than I was when I married Mel, and twelve years older than when I had my first kiss.

Norah screamed. It was long and loud and a pitch that I'd never heard before—the kind of scream I assume Rapunzel let out after being locked in a tower. It scared me. It must have scared Mel, too, because she came running into the living room to see if everything was all right.

"We're fine," I said. "Nothing to worry about here. I just told Norah about the boy monster in her mouth." I winked, assuming Mel would be as excited about this brilliant idea as I was.

"It's nothing," I said.

Norah started crying at my mention of the boy monster. She asked Mel to take it out. By now, six-year-old Tristan had entered the room. Even though he had no idea what a boy monster was, he started laughing at the sound of it.

"Boy monster," he said. "Monsters aren't boys."

Mel frowned. It was a confused and frustrated look that she often gives me when discovering one of my nonconventional parenting strategies, like the time I convinced Tristan to try broccoli because it would give him deadly farts.

Mel pulled me into the kitchen, Norah still crying on the sofa behind us, and I told her about the boy monster and how it couldn't be removed until Norah was twenty-eight years old.

"Isn't it wonderful?" I said.

Just the thought of it made me smile.

Norah had now moved from the sofa to the floor. She was sprawled out, right hand in her mouth, using her thumb and index finger to root around and pluck out the boy monster. Mel gave me a slack-jawed look and said, "What's wrong with you?" Then she walked into the kitchen, reached into Norah's mouth with two fingers, made a plucking motion, and said, "I got it."

Norah went slack with relief, while I groaned.

Later that night as I loaded the dishwasher,

Mel brought up the boy monster. She reminded me about how Tristan was kissed by a little girl at the park about two weeks earlier. We were at Silver Falls State Park with some friends. The daughter of one of our friends leaned over and kissed Tristan on the cheek. Then she ran away, squealing. She had red hair and dimples and was about a year younger and 3 inches (7.5 cm) taller than Tristan. She had to lean pretty far down to kiss him.

"What was your reaction then?" she asked.

I was silent. I didn't want to respond because I knew just where she was going.

"Oh. You don't remember? I'll tell you. You gave him a high five and called him a stallion." She stumbled saying "stallion," which seemed to give the word emphasis. "Then you told him that he takes after you."

She poked me in the chest.

"Which he does," I said with a wink, trying to make light of the situation but failing. Mel didn't laugh or contradict me. She just stayed on point.

"I don't understand the difference," Mel said. "Tristan gets a kiss and it's no big deal. In fact, you were happy about it. A boy kisses Norah, and you freak out."

I thought about it for a moment. I tried to defend myself with a bunch of false starts.

"But Tristan's a boy . . ."

"Norah's a girl . . ."

"Boys only want . . ."

But logically, none of my arguments added up. I could tell before I even finished saying them.

I stood next to the sink for a while, Mel staring at me, her eyes a mix of anger and curiosity. I tried to make sense of it. I searched deep inside to find a justification.

I looked at the ceiling, exhaled, and said, "I don't understand it either."

She kept looking at me, and finally I said it. "I'm sorry for telling Norah she had a boy monster in her mouth."

She nodded in a "that's right" sort of way. Then she said, "Don't apologize to me. Apologize to your daughter."

SHE KEPT LOOKING AT ME, AND FINALLY I SAID IT. "I'M SORRY FOR TELLING NORAH SHE HAD A BOY MONSTER IN HER MOUTH."

I told her I would, but naturally, it took a day to actually do it.

On Labor Day, we went to a park to barbecue with a large group of friends from church. Jonathon, the kissing boy, was there with his parents. He was dressed like Link—green pants, a green poncho, a long green hat, and a white shield in one hand and a sword in the other. Norah looked at him dreamily, and then the two went to the playground. Together they rode one of those big blue plastic seahorses on a large industrial spring.

The girl that kissed Tristan was there too. Her name was Susan. She sat on the lip of the sidewalk, elbows on her knees, face in her palms, and gazed at Tristan on the swing. He was screaming in his high-pitched little boy scream, legs kicking randomly, face red and distorted, clearly pandering for attention from Susan. Naturally, she was all about it, giggling as he did his thing.

I didn't get angry with Norah and I was not proud of Tristan. I just stood, stared, and accepted the fact that this was happening. I looked at Jonathon dressed as Link and thought to myself, *Norah. You could do better.*

But then I had one of those epiphanies fathers often have: *Who is actually good enough for my daughter?*

I couldn't think of anyone.

Later at the park, Norah sat next to me on a bench. She wrapped her soft hands around my forearm and hugged it like she often did.

"Why aren't you hanging out with Jonathon?" I asked.

She sighed and looked up at me. "He's playing swords with his friends. I don't like that game. It's stupid. I'm just going to sit by you."

And suddenly I had a realization. I'd gone through all of this anxiety over Norah and Jonathon. I had tried to intervene. But for what? Even at this young age, she could—and would—make decisions for herself. I didn't need to do a thing about it. I just needed to be there for her.

I put my arm around her, kissed the top of her head, and said, "I'm sorry I said you had a boy monster."

She looked up at me as if she'd totally forgot about the whole thing and shrugged. Then she grabbed me by the arm, dragged me to the playground, and together we rode a seesaw.

WHEN THE PARENTS ARE SICK AND THE KIDS ARE WELL, IT'S EVERY CHILD FOR THEMSELVES

Mel was in blue and white snowman pajama pants and a gray sweatshirt, curled into a ball on the living room floor of our small Minnesota townhome. Her brown hair was greasy and she smelled of BO and Pepto-Bismol. She gagged a little, and leaned forward, ready to sprint to the restroom, but then the gagging stopped and she slumped back down onto the floor and announced to the heavens, "I just want to die."

I was also in a ball, on the small, bluish-gray love seat in our living room, feeling much like how Mel looked and smelled, using everything I had to keep what was inside of me from getting out. Tristan was four and naked and standing on a white footstool at the bathroom sink. The water turned on and off, as he occasionally splashed it into his face and laughed. Even with the stool, he could hardly reach the faucet. His little arms, still round with baby fat, were high above his head, his toes the only thing touching the stool as he strained to fiddle with anything he could reach on the counter.

WHO KNEW WHAT HAPPENED TO HIS CLOTHING. I DIDN'T KNOW WHEN HE TOOK IT OFF. I DIDN'T EVEN KNOW HOW LONG HE'D BEEN NAKED.

He'd already pumped out all the *Finding Nemo* hand soap to make bubbles. They flowed out of the sink, and onto the counter, and along the cabinet door below like a bushy white beard. Before the soap, he'd been into the fruity Buzz Lightyear toothpaste. It coated his face, chest, stomach, arms—basically the whole front of his body—in blue war paint–like streaks. He'd painted the countertop with it, and some of the wall.

Who knew what happened to his clothing. I didn't know when he took it off. I didn't even know how long he'd been naked. I asked him to stop a few times, but once he realized I couldn't actually get up and physically stop him, he knew the day was his. I don't know what it is with four-year-olds and the bathroom sink, but whatever he was doing in there, it was clearly his Mona Lisa. Sure, he laughed, but he also kept making this high-pitched, nothing-can-beat-this-moment squeal, helping me know two things: (1) This was the most fun he'd ever had and (2) he was still alive. And frankly, in that moment, my children being alive was the bar.

SHE WAS RIPPING PAGES FROM BOOKS, AND TOSSING THE PAPER INTO THE AIR, AND SQUEALING AT ALMOST THE SAME PITCH AS HER OLDER BROTHER, AND ALL OF IT REMINDED ME OF THAT FIRST SCENE IN *GHOSTBUSTERS* WHEN THE DEAD LIBRARIAN SCREAMS AND STARTS THROWING INDEX CARDS.

Norah was in the living room, just out of Mel's reach. She was in nothing but a diaper that hung heavy between her legs, probably weighing somewhere near the 2-pound mark, but somehow it wasn't leaking. She was two, and she had taken all of the books out of every bookshelf. Every single one. I can't recall exactly how many bookshelves we had at the time, but I remember it being a lot. I was doing odd jobs at a children's book publisher, and they often gave me out-of-print editions, so to say that she pulled out all the books really doesn't capture the moment. There must have been close to 500 kids' books on the living room floor. She was ripping pages from them, and tossing the paper into the air, and squealing at almost the same pitch as her older brother, and all of it reminded me of that first scene in *Ghostbusters* when the dead librarian screams and starts throwing index cards.

A DVD of *The Backyardigans* was on repeat. It was a show about these animal-like things that had adventures in the backyard and sang songs, and we'd been watching the same half dozen episodes for who knows how long. Time didn't seem to function properly anymore. I had a difficult time determining the difference between night and day, and like Mel, I also wanted to die.

THE NIGHTS WERE LONG SHIFTS OF DOING LOAD AFTER LOAD OF LAUNDRY, SHAMPOOING THE CARPET, WASHING MY HANDS, AND WONDERING WHY I WENT TO COLLEGE ONLY TO BECOME MY CHILDREN'S PUKE SLAVE.

A few days earlier, Tristan started preschool. He came home with an *Angry Birds* backpack full of viruses. He threw up first. And naturally, he couldn't help but put his entire face inside his younger sister's face, giving her the virus. It was two days of begging both kids to puke in a bowl, only for them to throw up in heaving gasps down the front of their pajamas. The nights were long shifts of doing load after load of laundry, shampooing the carpet, washing my hands, and wondering why I went to college only to become my children's puke slave. The kids moaned and cried. I don't want to sound heartless, because I was totally there for them. I wanted them to get better, but ultimately, I didn't want them to touch me.

I didn't want this garbage in my body, but it didn't matter what I wanted. I had to hold them and comfort them, as they dry-heaved into every hole on my face. I don't know if I've ever used so much hand sanitizer in my life as I did before the onset of this illness. But looking back, I could have lubed my naked body in hand sanitizer, I could have drunk bleach, I could have lit my skin on fire, and I'd have still gotten sick.

It was inevitable.

MEL AND I HAD MANAGED WHAT SEEMED LIKE A MILLION FORMS OF THE PLAGUE AS PARENTS.

The moment the spring was back in our children's step, and they started begging for mac and cheese, and treats, and who knows what, Mel threw up. A few hours later, so did I.

Mel and I had managed what seemed like a million forms of the plague as parents. Before our move from Utah to Minnesota so that I could attend graduate school, there had always been a standard order of illness: I got sick or Mel got sick, and then the kids got sick. Or the kids got sick, and then one parent got sick, but the other was well enough to care for everyone. Or we lived close enough to family that we could get some backup from Mel's parents or my sister.

During my senior year of college, I came down with viral meningitis, which was easily the worst illness I'd ever experienced. But rather than stay home and take care of me, Mel got me to the doctor for a shot. Then Mel packed a bag for her and Tristan and moved in with her mother for a few days. And, sure, that sounds kind of cold, considering I'd pooped so much I started going blind. I can still remember the nurse asking me to drop my pants to give me a shot, and I looked her in the eyes and gave her this warning: "I've had diarrhea for sixteen hours. I'm not sure what it looks like back there." She gave me the shot anyway because nurses are obviously saints.

But on the whole, I understood Mel's actions. She called and checked on me a couple of times a day. Sometimes she left me soup on the doorstep. But let's be real, I'd have also turned our home into a quarantine zone if Mel had come down with that same illness.

Before this viral death spiral in Minnesota, there had always been at least one competent adult able to help the well children. But this time, it was the perfect storm.

Mel and I came down with the same illness at almost the exact same time, and both of our very young and active children were now immune to that virus. We had no family nearby. We had a few friends, but we didn't feel close enough to any of them to invite them into our virus-filled hell home. And this wasn't an average, tough-it-out sort of illness. This was an evacuation-at-every-end, I-can't-move-without-my-body-revolting, what-bioweapons-lab-did-this-originate-in sort of illness. So we just had to lie on the floor and let it pass, doing the bare minimum for our children, napping in shifts, and keeping one eye on the kids just enough to make sure they didn't kill themselves.

The rules didn't apply anymore. There were no TV limits. There were no more healthy lunches or fights over eating so many bites before having a dessert. They could do what they wanted in any room of the house. No one could stop them. Mel and I couldn't stand up long enough to cook anything without throwing up, and the smell of food was intolerable, so Tristan and Norah ate what they could reach.

I can remember Tristan having a can of Pepsi and some marshmallows for breakfast. Then he told me his tummy hurt at the exact moment I was throwing up in a plastic bag. I had zero sympathy for him. Norah took a few bites from a block of cheese and washed it down with a SlimFast shake. That was her breakfast. Outside of Tristan's short-lived tummyache, neither child complained about these meals, which I will say was a refreshing change, considering they viewed every home-cooked healthy meal we made as a personal attack.

Near lunchtime, I was curled up on our love seat. Tristan was sitting on my right arm with a full bag of nacho cheese DORITOS®, eating joyfully and wiping his hand on my T-shirt. Norah sat on the side of my right leg eating a box of cookies, dusting me and our sofa with crumbs.

As if the smell of Tristan's chips weren't bad enough, he kept trying to offer me some. I say "offer" loosely because he was four—in reality, he more or less tried to cram chips into my mouth. I didn't have the strength to fight him off, so I just clinched my lips and begged him to stop, making me sound like some sort of an angry, grumbling ventriloquist dummy. A sound that my son found hilarious.

For Mel and me, this had to have been the worst twelve hours of our parenting lives. But in contrast, for Norah and Tristan, it was potentially the best twelve hours they'd ever experienced.

No one took a bath and no one was forced to wash their hands. Were Mel and I dying? Well . . . aren't we all? But in the very literal sense, while we wanted to die, we weren't actually dying. However, we very clearly didn't have the strength to parent. I couldn't believe how quickly our children changed into cheese-block munching, chip-force-eating, freethinking anarchists.

There's this scene in *Breaking Bad* where Jesse spends the night with some meth-addicted parents. The house is a mess and their little boy more or less takes care of himself, and you cannot look at that episode without feeling total empathy for the poor child. When I look back on the time Mel and I got the virus after our children, it feels a lot like that episode. If Child Protective Services had dropped in for a surprise visit, I have no doubt they'd have assumed Mel and I were drug addicts and taken away our children. I don't know if I've ever felt so ashamed of myself as a father.

But I suppose these are the moments that give parenting range, right? This was the new low for us, and much of it was the situation and little of it had to do with how we acted on a good day.

During the height of my fever, as Tristan worked his toothpaste art in the bathroom and Norah tore apart our books, Mel looked at me and said, "We must be the worst parents ever."

I looked back at her, went to say something comforting, but then had to sprint to the restroom to throw up. Between the water, soap, and toothpaste on the floor, I slipped and fell, slamming my head into the wall. I lay on the ground for a bit, seeing stars and dry-heaving.

Mel asked if I was okay from the living room, and I said, "Yeah, I think so."

Then Tristan did something I didn't expect. He shut off the water, got off his stool, and crouched over me.

"Where does it hurt?" he asked.

I sat up and pointed to the back of my head, where I could already feel a nice goose egg forming.

He walked around me and kissed my head, then tugged me by the arm into the living room. He laid me down on the sofa, covering me with a blanket. He rubbed his soapy, toothpaste-covered hand through my hair, and said, "Poor little guy. You must be really sick. I take'a care of you."

All of it was exactly what I'd done for him a few days earlier, when he was the sick one. Despite all the poor parenting I'd done that day, watching my son mimic the way I took care of him was pretty adorable.

Across the room, Norah was snuggled up against her mother, both of them sleeping on the floor. Tristan went into his bedroom, tugged the quilt off of his own bed, and then put it over them. Then he crawled beneath it as well and went to sleep. I didn't know what time it was, but it was dark outside, so I assumed the three of them were down for the night.

By morning, the worst of it had past, and Mel and I felt good enough to parent again.

As I gave Tristan a bath, I told him thanks for kissing my head and getting the family a blanket. He looked up at me with a sly grin and said, "You just'a needed my help."

"Yeah, I did," I said. "Where did you learn to be such a good helper?"

He shrugged, and then looked up at me with this bright, sparse-toothed grin that seemed to say, "You."

KIDS! STOP
BEING GROSS.

I was going through Tristan's sock drawer when I realized that his *Harry Potter* socks, and *Legend of Zelda* socks, and taco print socks, and, well, every single pair of socks he owned had white, dried, salty sweat lines. He didn't own any regular white, black, or brown socks anymore. Every sock had to be a little extra, and every extra sock, as I observed, smelled extra too.

Like really extra.

It was one of those overwhelming body odor smells that I'd only smelled once before, when I found a gym bag full of my used gym clothes that I'd left in the garage for days and days until it became something new and horrible and would probably register as a life-form on Mars.

I gagged then, and I'm gagging a little now as I write about it.

Tristan was probably ten or eleven—just old enough to smell like adolescence.

Per my job as his father, I asked him why all the socks in his dresser smelled like death, and he said with an I'm-really-nailing-this-hygiene-thing confidence, "You told me to change my socks every day."

IT WAS ONE OF THOSE OVERWHELMING BODY ODOR SMELLS THAT I'D ONLY SMELLED ONCE BEFORE, WHEN I FOUND A GYM BAG FULL OF MY USED GYM CLOTHES THAT I'D LEFT IN THE GARAGE FOR DAYS AND DAYS UNTIL IT BECAME SOMETHING NEW AND HORRIBLE AND WOULD PROBABLY REGISTER AS A LIFE-FORM ON MARS.

He was wearing a blue zip-up hoodie with grease stains the width of his fingers across the chest and crumbs below the chin and along the zipper, a pair of black adidas track pants with three white stripes up the legs and a small hole in the right knee. Beneath the jacket was a gray T-shirt with the cover of *Harry Potter and the Deathly Hallows*. I knew this because it was the same shirt he wore every single day unless I insisted he change it. Then he'd wear a blue T-shirt with a picture of a black and white dabbing cat that read, "Dab Cat."

I called this his "outfit" because he insisted on wearing it 24-7. Not that he didn't have other clothing options. He did. He had a closet and a dresser full of varying, clean, ready-to-be-worn outfits with the same characters, books, and video game themes as his socks. And yes, he had to change out of the outfit for school. He attended a charter school, and they had a dress code, forcing him to slide into khaki shorts and a red school polo. And on Sunday I made him wear slacks, a white shirt, and a tie to church. But any other moment in his life—evenings, weekends, holidays, sleep—he wore the "outfit."

BUT TRYING TO EXPLAIN A PRETEEN'S OBSESSIONS AND ODD HABITS FEELS LIKE TRYING TO EXPLAIN DONALD TRUMP'S TWITTER FEED.

Why? I don't know. It's not like it was anything special. But trying to explain a preteen's obsessions and odd habits feels like trying to explain Donald Trump's Twitter feed. Some of it was logical, even humorous, but a lot of it wasn't. Once a week, I'd pry the "outfit" off his body, soak it in stain remover, and wash it. You'd think I actually removed his skin. I once missed a week because I didn't feel up to fighting with him. It was a bad decision because I now know what it smells like to shove my face into an armpit.

Tristan smiled up at me as we discussed his sock drawer. There was orange food in his teeth.

Probably *Goldfish*® crackers.

"Okay," I said. "That's correct, I did tell you to change your socks every day." Then I waited for him to explain this whole smelly sock situation. But he didn't. He just went about his business as if the conversation was over, so I probed a little more, asking him to further explain his sock-changing routine.

"In the morning," he said, "I put on new socks, and put the old ones back in the drawer."

I'VE MADE SOME STUPID ASSUMPTIONS AS A PARENT, BUT I SUPPOSE THE WINNER RIGHT THERE AND THEN WAS THAT MY PRETEEN UNDERSTOOD THAT DIRTY SOCKS GO IN THE HAMPER.

Then he shrugged like it was just a thing. Nothing to see here. I was left, once again, feeling like I was failing in my attempts to turn my son into a socially acceptable human who didn't make the world blurry with stink lines.

I've made some stupid assumptions as a parent, but I suppose the winner right there and then was that my preteen understood that dirty socks go in the hamper. I also now understood why, when he took his shoes off as I drove him home from soccer practice, I had to roll all the windows down and practically stick my head out the van window.

To his credit, he was doing what I'd asked him to do to some regard. He was just missing one critical step.

As I informed him that dirty socks go in the

hamper, he looked at me as if asking him to add this one critical step to his routine was how society breaks down. I couldn't help but reflect on how long I'd been failing at teaching him how to not be gross.

As long as I'd known the boy, he'd been comfortable with his own filth. Boogers? Not a problem. BO? Nothing to be concerned with. Burps, farts, poop? Why get worked up about any of that? It felt like the part of his mind that was concerned with his own cleanliness had been crosswired. I didn't understand why I had to ask Tristan if he used soap in the shower, only for him to say, "I forgot." I didn't understand why I had to ask him if he changed his underwear, only for him to ask, "Why?"

Sometimes it felt like I was teaching this horribly complex thing, like how to find a wormhole in space, when it really shouldn't be that complicated. Right?

I DIDN'T UNDERSTAND WHY I HAD TO ASK HIM IF HE CHANGED HIS UNDERWEAR, ONLY FOR HIM TO ASK, "WHY?"

Lather, rinse, repeat. There isn't all that much to it.

But with my son, it all seemed so complicated.

I mean, I suppose teaching him about hygiene

wasn't a complete wash. Some of my lessons stuck, but many of them didn't, and for each lesson he learned, he seemed to develop two new nasty habits—something similar to cutting heads off of Hydra, only not nearly as heroic and twice as nasty.

People talk a lot about showing your children that you love them, but they don't always go into the specifics. Well, here's a fact: Teaching my son how to not be gross was the purest show of love in the history of parenting.

A few years before the socks, we were working in the yard together, and he ate a booger in front of me.

Then he smiled and said, "Mmmmm."

"You know, Tristan," I said, "someday you're going to do that in front of someone you're attracted to. That person is going to call you disgusting, while you are going to think they're cute. It will make you feel so crappy that you won't ever eat a booger again."

I assumed he would tell me that I was lying. That he didn't care who liked him or not, or some other cliché kid answer. Instead, Tristan looked up at me, hands dirty from pulling weeds, the booger still soaking in his mouth, and said, "Did you ever eat a booger in front of Mom?"

I laughed. "No," I said. "But I ate a booger in front of a girl on the school bus once. It wasn't your mom. Her name was Liz. I thought this girl was really cute at the time, and I thought eating a booger would make her laugh like it did with my buddies. I was probably ten. I put the booger in my mouth, and then showed it to her, just like you did, and she threw up in her lap."

Tristan didn't look shocked after my confession. He didn't come across as moved or anything even close to it. Instead, he put his hand over his little chubby tummy and laughed long and hard. "That's awesome!" he exclaimed.

I shook my head and said, "No, it wasn't. It was embarrassing."

Then I told him about when I was older, and how I liked a girl in junior high. We were starting to get along until I farted on her leg. I thought I was being charming, but she obviously didn't feel the same way because she kicked me in the balls. I told him a couple more embarrassing stories that I still cringe about at 4:00 a.m.

"Listen," I said. "Someday, you're going to grow up and be on your own. You will probably get married to someone you really love and respect. And my advice to you is, don't be gross or you will never find that special person. Be a gentleman. Treat your partner with respect. If you don't, it will make your partner feel like they are the kind of person who doesn't deserve respect. And that's not a way to make a good relationship work."

Neither of us spoke for a moment.

Then Tristan said, "Okay." It wasn't sarcastic, or frustrated, or insecure. It was real, and once again, I felt hopeful.

But I must say, this was my life with a little boy.

Wait, that kind of singles out one gender, and I know that little girls can be gross too. Heck, all children can be gross. Some boys are really clean. My nephew was like that. He was one of those "I have several bottles of cologne and I'm only eight," fancy-schmancy kind of boys that wore polos and button-up shirts to the playground. Not that I was expecting Tristan to be Richie Rich, or worse, a Kardashian. I just wanted to be able to hug him and not feel like I needed a shower.

Tristan's journey to becoming a hygienic human has been in short, incremental steps; something that seemed so obvious simply wasn't. And each time it happened, I wondered if I was doing it wrong, and with each step along the way, I couldn't help but look back at my own life and realize that I was exactly that nasty.

TRISTAN'S JOURNEY TO BECOMING A HYGIENIC HUMAN HAS BEEN IN SHORT, INCREMENTAL STEPS; SOMETHING THAT SEEMED SO OBVIOUS SIMPLY WASN'T.

The fact that I eventually figured it out should have given me some hope, but I don't know if any of that makes it any easier to live with someone who may, at any moment, burp and blow it in your face.

But what I can say is that the day I told Tristan about how his dirty socks needed to go in the hamper, we were packing a bag to go camping. It was going to be just the two of us.

That night, as we sat in the tent playing a game on the iPad before going to bed, I noticed a pair of dirty socks at the bottom of the tent.

"What's that?" I asked.

"Those are my dirty socks."

"Wait," I began. "What are you planning to do with them?"

"I'm going to put them in the hamper like you said."

I paused for a moment. Then I asked, "Did you just mention the hamper?"

He gave me a stern side-eye.

It was a small tent, so I was right next to him. He was still in the "outfit," sure, but as he spoke, I noticed a minty freshness.

"Did you brush your teeth?" I asked.

He looked at me with a flat face that seemed to say, "Duh."

Then I took a sniff near his chest, "Are you wearing deodorant?"

"Yes," he said. "I always do."

I leaned in closer for another sniff, and he pushed my face away.

"What are you doing?" he asked.

"You smell good."

I sat there for a moment and realized it might

have been the first time I'd said that to my son since his new-baby smell. I took one more sniff just to savor the moment, and he shoved my face away and said I was being "weird."

MY USE OF SLANG IS EMBARRASSING

I stay cool by keeping up with the slang, yo. But each year I get a little closer to 40, and I get more and more excited about lawn care. I think a lot about my mortgage and I buy my pants at Costco. I'm a nerdy father to the core, trying to be cool but failing pretty hard. When I was 19, I was wearing a Black Flag shirt, and this guy close to the age I am now pulled up his sleeve to show me his Black Flag tattoo. He gave me this wrinkle-faced, coffee-stained smile that said, "I'm still relevant." I looked at him like he came to America on the *Mayflower*. The look I gave him is the exact look my preteen son gives me each time I say, "YOLO." There's so much slang I just don't get, but I try to, and ultimately I end up embarrassing myself—and most importantly, my preteen son.

Here are a few examples.

According to Urban Dictionary, "yeet" is used to express excitement. I must've heard Tristan say "yeet" a million times, but the moment I said, "Check it out, dude! I'm going to yeet my multivitamin," Tristan stopped using it.

Tristan was watching a YouTuber and the dude kept screaming, "My boi," which I later learned means a good friend. I screamed, "My boi" as Tristan entered his school's Christmas performance and his eyes got all glossy and angry and I'm pretty sure he's going to find some way to give me COVID-19.

I learned all about YOLO ("you only live once") during a National Public Radio story about up-and-coming slang, which is probably the dorkiest, most fatherly place to learn about slang outside of reading about it on a box of oat bran. Plus, the fact that it was being discussed on NPR means it already wasn't cool anymore. Not that any of that stopped me from screaming, "Tristan, use your YOLO!" at his soccer game or prevented him from actually tripping over my crappy use of pop culture phrasing.

I work at a university, and some of the college students told me that "whip" means a nice car. As Tristan rode the skateboard I got him, I complimented his "sweet whip." I even winked. His friends laughed at me. They laughed good and hard, and the whole time Tristan looked at me with red-faced horror.

While dropping Tristan off for school, I called his name. As he looked back, I extended my right arm, bent the left across my face, and lowered my head, in what could only be described as an epic dab being performed in the front seat of our minivan. His shoulders went so slack that his backpack fell. One of his buddies called me a "chongus." I looked it up on my phone in the school's parking lot. It means "someone who dabs for no good reason and enjoys annoying people." I ordered a coffee mug that read "chongus."

Tristan was teaching me how to play Minecraft and he called me a "noob." I didn't say anything because I didn't have any idea what he meant. I quietly went online and found out that being a "noob" meant that I was new to something, which I will admit, was accurate. So he wasn't insulting me, necessarily. The real insult, however, was when I called Tristan a noob as I was teaching him how to use a power drill. He asked me how I knew what the word meant, and I said, "I looked it up." He rolled his eyes—he rolled them real hard—and said, "Dad! You Urban Dictionaried it!" I looked that term up. Here's the definition: "What your mother did to find out what you meant."

Tristan told me he was "grinding" with his friend at school, and I paused. Back in the '90s, "grinding" meant to make out with someone real hard while grinding your . . . well . . . you get the idea.

"The school allows you to do that?" I asked

"Yeah," he said. "Why wouldn't they?"

"I'm just surprised," I said.

He told me it was with his buddy Jason. They were grinding really hard in algebra, and as he spoke, I started to get a little dizzy because I just wasn't ready for this sort of thing.

Then he triumphantly said, "We finished three math assignments!"

I asked him what he thought "grinding" meant, and he told me, "You know, to work really hard on something. What did you think it meant?"

I didn't answer. I just complimented him on his grind.

See? I'm trying and failing with the slang. But last Thanksgiving, Tristan and I played football in the morning with some friends from church. We were on the same team. Tristan was the quarterback, and he passed me the ball. I caught it in the end zone. It was an epic father-and-son play, and as I spiked the ball, Tristan screamed, "My boi!" I knew exactly what he meant, and it may have been the coolest I've felt since before flannel went out of style.

THE

INTERROGATION

There was yellow around the toilet bolts and along the side of the bowl. Yellow was splashed on the seat because it obviously hadn't been put up. There was a line of yellow along the wall, and a small puddle was slowly drying on the linoleum. I don't know how much a young boy's bladder holds. It could be ounces or liters or gallons, but what I do know is that it looked a lot like how I imagined a fire station looked when a firehose lights up without a fireman attached.

We had two bathrooms. One for the kids and one for the adults.

I was in the kids' bathroom.

Someone was going to have to clean it up, and I'd have preferred it to be whoever made this impressive pee-pee mess. The hope here was to make lemonade out of lemons. Was that a bad analogy when talking about pee? Yes. It was. The point is that by making the guilty party clean up their own mess, they would hopefully stop making messes. Perhaps better control their pee parts, and stop making the whole house smell like a rest home.

Not that anything was ever as simple as A + B = C with parenting.

The real tricky part here was going to be getting the confession.

SOMEONE WAS GOING TO HAVE TO CLEAN IT UP, AND I'D HAVE PREFERRED IT TO BE WHOEVER MADE THIS IMPRESSIVE PEE-PEE MESS.

In my experience thus far, 60 percent of parenting had come down to solving a whodunit mystery. Evidence was always plentiful, but confessions were next to impossible. I never thought I'd become a "detective" when I got into this whole parenting gig, but I seemed to be constantly interrogating my children, lining them up and trying to figure out who did what, where, and how as each one of them pointed at a sibling, or the dog, or the neighbor, or God, or the fates—anyone or anything, really—in a desperate attempt to never, ever take credit for their own bad behavior.

Not that this was a new tactic in the legacy of childhood. I blamed everything on my older brother, and in turn, he blamed everything on me. Not that we ever coordinated this effort. It happened organically. But each time we refused to take responsibility for something, which was often, we knew we had at least a 50 percent chance of our parents giving up, and their investigation would drift off into the ether with no charges being filed. But to be real, if we'd just harnessed our powers for good and stopped doing stupid things—and when we did, fessed up to our actions and moved along—we'd have spent less time trapped in our room, missing dinner, our parents trying to starve out a confession.

But naturally, I didn't think that way as a child, and neither did my kids. Nothing was worse than getting in trouble for something you actually did. That mentality is born into children, and it is in direct contrast with my obligations as a father to stick it to my children and teach them accountability.

Naturally, my first and only suspect was Tristan, who was seven and the only person in the family built to pee like a jerk. Well, outside of me, but I knew for a fact I didn't make the mess because I went out of my way to avoid using the kids' restroom, because regardless of how much we cleaned it, I couldn't walk in there and not feel like it was where Ebola originated.

This should have been an open-and-close case, but if I'd learned anything about raising children up to this point, it's that if I accused Tristan of something and he didn't admit to it, he'd end up resenting me, and I'd end up with this horrible feeling that I may have convicted my son of a crime he didn't commit. Sure, this wasn't *Making a Murderer* or anything like that. But if I wanted my son to resent me instead of acknowledging his wrong and making a lasting change in his behavior, making him clean the restroom without a confession was a surefire way to get there.

NOTHING WAS WORSE THAN GETTING IN TROUBLE FOR SOMETHING YOU ACTUALLY DID. THAT MENTALITY IS BORN INTO CHILDREN, AND IT IS IN DIRECT CONTRAST WITH MY OBLIGATIONS AS A FATHER TO STICK IT TO MY CHILDREN AND TEACH THEM ACCOUNTABILITY.

I found Tristan in the kitchen, eating Lucky Charms and playing on the iPad. Perhaps "eating Lucky Charms" was a stretch. To be more specific, he was eating the marshmallows out of a bowl of Lucky Charms, something that made me totally crazy because there were regularly bowls of marshmallow-less Lucky Charms all over our house that no one wanted to eat, because what would be the point? Marshmallows are life.

"Dude. Did you pee all over the toilet?"

He gave me this guilty, eyes-wide, slack-jawed look. Then he buttoned it up and gave me a tighter-lipped, puppy dog–eyed look of innocence.

"No! I didn't pee all over the place," Tristan said.

He was nervous.

He was trembling.

He was suspicious.

He started to speak in nonsense. "I don't . . . even pee. I mean . . . I haven't peed today. It was probably Norah."

"Really, Tristan? All day?"

I started my integration.

"It's 2:00 p.m. And Norah isn't equipped to do that kind of damage."

Tristan and I went back and forth for a while, but he was quickly running out of explanations. He tried blaming it on his mother, which was a little shocking. He tried blaming it on me, which I wasn't having.

Eventually he exclaimed, "It was Taran!"

Taran was the neighbor boy who spent most of his free time at our house. And indeed, he'd sat in our living room earlier that morning. I thought I had Tristan pinned until that moment. This Taran explanation really spoiled my interrogation. And today, I'm proud of his ability to find an alternative. It showed his unwillingness to back down. But at the time, I was angry because I thought I had him.

"You know what, it was either you or Taran," I said. "Taran is your friend. That means his pee is your responsibility."

Tristan gave me a terrified look because he knew I had him. And it was only then, when he had no wiggle room, that he finally admitted it was, indeed, him.

"Get in there and clean it up," I said.

"I can't clean it up," he said. "I don't know how."

"I'm *not* cleaning up your pee," I said. "You are old enough to handle your own mess."

I TOLD HER WHAT HAPPENED AS IF I WERE SOME GREAT CRIMINAL DETECTIVE. I TOLD HER ABOUT THE INTERROGATION, HOW I'D NAILED TRISTAN. AND NOW HE WAS CLEANING THE TOILET AND LEARNING A VALUABLE LESSON ABOUT LIFE AND MARRIAGE AND PEEING PROPERLY.

I set him up with a toilet brush, some cleaner, and some gloves. I told him what to do. I lectured him for a bit. I gloated, but only slightly. I told him that if he didn't figure out how to pee in the toilet now, his future spouse was going to leave him. I told him I was doing him a favor. I leaned against the bathroom door frame, well up on my soapbox as he cleaned.

Mel came home from the store around this time. I don't know how long she stood in the kitchen listening to me, but once she came down the hall, I walked with her into our bedroom.

I told her what happened as if I were some great criminal detective. I told her about the interrogation, how I'd nailed Tristan. And now he was cleaning the toilet and learning a valuable lesson about life and marriage and peeing properly.

I smiled with satisfaction.

I assumed she'd be proud of me.

Mel gave me a curt smile, and then she asked me to follow her into our restroom. I asked her why, but she didn't respond—she just took my hand in an insistent sort of way.

Once we were next to our toilet, she pointed at the floor near the front of the bowl. There was a small half-dried pool of pee, about the size of a silver dollar.

Suddenly it was my turn to be interrogated. Or perhaps it was just an accusation.

She didn't exactly ask questions because we both knew I was guilty.

"I found it this morning!" she said. "You are just as gross as your son. Actually, you are probably worse, because you're thirty-one and he's seven."

I wanted to stand up for myself. I wanted to blame Tristan. If we'd had a dog at this time, I'd have probably blamed it. I wanted to tell her that I didn't turn on the light in the night so that I wouldn't wake her, and that's why I didn't hit the bowl. But really, I just didn't try hard enough the night before, so I didn't say anything.

I was busted.

Mel left the room, and as she walked down the hall, she stopped at the kids' bathroom and said, "Tristan, thank you for cleaning up your mess.

Now please bring the toilet brush to your father. He has a mess of his own to clean up."

Moments later, Tristan stood in the restroom doorway, still sporting yellow cleaning gloves, the toilet brush in one hand and some bowl cleaner in the other. He handed them to me. We shared a glance, and as strange as it sounds, it felt like we were sharing something more. An embarrassment that could only be shared by a father and son.

I TALKED TO MY DAUGHTER ABOUT BODY IMAGE, AND OH MAN . . . I BLEW IT!

We were driving to see a movie when I asked Norah why she'd been calling herself fat recently. We were on a daddy-daughter date. I assumed body image would come up eventually, but I didn't expect it at age nine.

It was Mel who told me about it. She worked at our daughter's school. One day during recess, she overheard Norah, along with her two friends, talking about how they were fat and needed to lose weight. Not that the shape of my daughter defined her, but if you were to actually look for her, she would have easily been missed. She was the shortest in her third-grade class, her arms and legs like skinny ropes. Were she to try and lose weight, I wasn't sure where it would've come from.

That was the really dangerous part. Her view of herself was clearly skewed to make this small adorable girl think that she was fat, and I worried that it was going to also impact her overall health and development if she did try to lose weight. And yet, here we were, my daughter discussing her weight as if it were a concern, when what I wanted her to be doing was playing hide-and-seek, or tag, or discussing how all the boys in her class were gross. You know, regular nine-year-old stuff.

But instead she was discussing something new and scary that neither Mel nor I felt prepared for.

AND YET, HERE WE WERE, MY DAUGHTER DISCUSSING HER WEIGHT AS IF IT WERE A CONCERN, WHEN WHAT I WANTED HER TO BE DOING WAS PLAYING HIDE-AND-SEEK, OR TAG, OR DISCUSSING HOW ALL THE BOYS IN HER CLASS WERE GROSS. YOU KNOW, REGULAR NINE-YEAR-OLD STUFF.

Mel broached the subject with Norah and didn't get anywhere. For the most part Norah just shut down, so Mel asked me to give it a shot during our daddy-daughter date.

It was evening, and we were on a dark, winding, wooded road between our small Oregon town and another, just the two of us in the van. I waited for her to respond to my question, and when she didn't after a long stretch of silence, I just started talking.

Is "talking" the right word?

Perhaps I should say I word vomited.

I went on for some time.

I used "beautiful" and "pretty" and "charming" and "intelligent" and "funny" to describe her. I said how far she was from being fat. I told her that the shape of her body didn't define her, or anyone for that matter. I tried so hard to describe her from my perspective, as someone who had held her at birth, and watched her walk and talk and learn. I wanted her to see how much I've learned about real love and understanding from raising her and how I knew, without a doubt, that she was truly something special in the world.

I talked for a while.

The funny thing is, I had this all planned out in my head before we got in the van. It was a script, really. In my mind, it all went so smoothly. I was going to tell her how I saw her, and I just knew she'd nod along, totally understanding what I was saying, and never again see herself as fat, or unattractive, or anything other than the charming, wonderful daughter I see every single day.

But in the moment, it just came out as a stammering, steaming pile of short half-sentences, me not sure what to say but just letting it out, the whole time feeling this pit in my stomach and knowing that I wanted to get this right—but it didn't feel right, not even a little right. Ultimately, I didn't know exactly what right looked like, so I just kept talking.

I was midsentence when Norah screamed into the passenger window, "I don't want to talk about it!"

THIS MAY HAVE BEEN THE MOST OVERWHELMING MOMENT OF MY FATHERHOOD, AND I'LL TELL YOU WHY. IT IS SO HEARTBREAKING TO LOOK AT SOMEONE WHO YOU FIND TO BE ABSOLUTELY WONDERFUL, IN ALL ASPECTS OF EVERYTHING, AND HAVE THEM FEEL LIKE THEY'RE NOT.

It got quiet except for the sounds of the road.

And I felt it in my hands and toes.

I felt it in my heart.

I felt it in every part of me.

I'd blown it, and I worried that I'd just made things worse.

Up until that moment, I felt confident that if I told her how I really felt about her, I could change the way she saw herself.

But it didn't work.

This may have been the most overwhelming moment of my fatherhood, and I'll tell you why. It is so heartbreaking to look at someone who you find to be absolutely wonderful, in all aspects of everything, and have them feel like they're not. It's a dark feeling, a helpless feeling, one that I didn't know existed until that moment in the van.

I didn't know what else to say.

Norah was obviously done talking, so I dropped it, and we drove to the theater in this swampy, uncomfortable silence, her looking out the window and me looking at the road.

By the time we made it to the theater we were back to normal, talking like the conversation never happened. That made me even more nervous, because it made me feel like she'd already learned how to bury those feelings about herself deep inside—and I had no idea how to change that.

I came home, and Mel asked how it went, so I told her. Then I ended with, "So . . . not well." We talked about our pasts and any issues we'd had with body image in an attempt to figure out if the way we overcame a similar challenge could work for our daughter. Mel told me that she didn't have body issues until after children: "I feel like I'm in competition with my younger self. I just can't get back there." We ordered some books online that we thought might help. Then Mel said something profound.

"You compliment me every day, and it helps. I fight with you about it, but it helps." She went on to say that whatever was happening outside of our house that was making our daughter feel this way about herself was, for the most part, out of our control. "But what we can do right now is try to build her up while she's here."

So we made a pact to compliment Norah each day on who she was, who she was becoming, and how much value she brought to our house and us.

"What bothers me the most," I said, "is that I know she's truly something special. I think she's so adorable and smart and everything I could ask for in a daughter. I just can't stand her not seeing herself that way." I went on for a moment more, talking about how much I admire Norah. I said all the things I wanted to say in the van, only this time it came out the way I wanted it to.

"I feel the same," Mel said.

We were quiet for a moment, and it felt like someone was watching us. It was after 9:00 p.m. and all the kids were in bed, but when I turned around, Norah was standing in the hallway wearing green and yellow flower print pajamas.

Mel and I looked at each other, and then we looked at our daughter. Her eyes were a little misty, and I wasn't sure what to make of that. I worried she was going to come at us with anger because she felt we were talking behind her back.

She ran into the room and hugged me around the waist. It was one of those deep hugs, the tight ones that parents don't get nearly enough of. The ones that say, "I need you."

Mel swooped in from the side, and all three of us just hugged one another. It was one of those moments I didn't expect but was grateful for. I knew this didn't completely change the way Norah saw herself. I knew that she'd probably still struggle with body image for years to come because that is the sad reality of right here and right now. But I also felt confident that at the very least, she understood that she had two parents who really loved her and saw her value.

We stopped hugging.

I leaned down and kissed the top of Norah's head. Then I picked her up and carried her back to bed, her arms around my neck, squeezing me tightly.

GET THIS . . .
HE WAS ACTUALLY
LISTENING THE
WHOLE TIME!

I was organizing a few things in the garage when Tristan announced that he was heading to the park with some friends from the neighborhood. This was shortly after his 12th birthday. Right before he left, I looked him in the eyes and softly said, "Remember what we talked about." Then I shifted my gaze to the pimple-faced kid waiting in our driveway who lived down the street from us. I'd often overheard that boy spouting all sorts of swears and nastiness while also being a total jack wagon to other kids in the neighborhood. I didn't actually know his name. I mean, I'd heard it, but I kept forgetting it, so I just called him Jack Wagon Kid, mostly to myself, because it's rude to call kids names when you're an adult even when you really want to.

Anyway, he was a bit of a foulmouthed bully. Tristan had mentioned that Jack Wagon Kid made him feel uncomfortable. He insisted that I couldn't speak to the kid's parents about any of this, or Jack Wagon Kid directly, because it would be embarrassing. It was a request I upheld because I understood his predicament. But I must admit it was difficult—I really wanted to give that Jack Wagon Kid a sharp kick right in the butthole.

The park was just down the street from our house, and all three boys left on their bikes, with baseball mitts on the handlebars. I watched them pull out and ride down the street, looking like they were in a scene from *The Sandlot*. And like any father does in a situation like this, I felt a little nervous.

BUT I MUST ADMIT IT WAS DIFFICULT—I REALLY WANTED TO GIVE THAT JACK WAGON KID A SHARP KICK RIGHT IN THE BUTTHOLE.

In true dad fashion, I must have given Tristan a million gold nuggets of advice by this point. I'd poured all of my wisdom into that little boy, and for all intents and purposes, he appeared to be rejecting it with the same gaggy enthusiasm he did with the vast majority of our healthy homemade meals. I acknowledge that as a preteen, I did the same thing. I assumed all adults were (1) stupid, (2) out to get me, (3) out of touch, and (4) chronically in need of a breath mint.

But now, as a grown man, I can just look at my children and make predictions about their behavior or life choices, and I'm 95 percent right. And it's not hard to do. I mean, come on. How hard is it to look at a kid huffing down a pillowcase full of candy on Halloween and not know they are going to throw up in the night?

I'D POURED ALL OF MY WISDOM INTO THAT LITTLE BOY, AND FOR ALL INTENTS AND PURPOSES, HE APPEARED TO BE REJECTING IT WITH THE SAME GAGGY ENTHUSIASM HE DID WITH THE VAST MAJORITY OF OUR HEALTHY HOMEMADE MEALS.

I give my advice. It's rejected. I am left to just let my kids do all the stupid things that go against my warnings, and ultimately I end up washing their puke-filled bedsheets at two o'clock in the morning while grumbling under my breath, "I told you so."

My advice on how to handle this neighborhood bully was no different. The day before Tristan left for the park, I'd told him that if Jack Wagon Kid made him feel uncomfortable or placed him in a bad situation, he needed to stand up and ask him to stop. And if he didn't, he should leave. Simple solution. As I spoke, he nodded absentmindedly, then he shrugged and everything about his countenance made me feel like I was interrupting something important.

And let's put something on the table right now. I knew how to handle this kid because frankly, I had held a number of similar traits as a child. Back in the day, I was the kid swearing and talking in nasties. I was the kid who was two steps from being sent to the alternative high school for making tasteless jokes in class. I was the one who got banned from coming over by my friend's parents for calling someone a "douche" for not passing the mashed potatoes. Don't get me wrong. I certainly wasn't a bully like Jack Wagon Kid. I didn't pick on anyone. I also wasn't a criminal, exactly. I don't think I was destined for prison. I was more like the devil's helper, you know. A Bart Simpson type.

I KNEW HOW TO HANDLE THIS KID BECAUSE FRANKLY, I HAD HELD A NUMBER OF SIMILAR TRAITS AS A CHILD.

But the sad reality was that most who knew me as a teen assumed I was destined for prison. I ran away from home when I was fourteen. I started experimenting with drugs around that time too. I eventually went to live with my grandmother, who saved my life.

But there's something about coming from a broken home and being that troubled child with a troubled drug-addicted father, that child who lived with his grandmother, that caused everyone—teachers, parents, friends—to assume that I was predestined to fail at life. This was the shadow I lived beneath as a child, and it made me wonder if I was destined to fail as a father too. It was that same shadow of predestined failure that made me hesitant to get married and even more hesitant to have children.

Thinking back, the choice to have a child was probably one of the biggest arguments Mel and I ever had. She wanted children bad, and I did too. But I was also weighted with this horrible feeling that I didn't have it in me to be a good dad because I didn't have a good dad. I'd spent most of my childhood assuming I was going to be a failure at all things, and it made me feel like I shouldn't bring a child into that mess.

It took Mel a couple of years of convincing me that I could, in fact, be a decent dad, and that my troubled childhood and my father's drug addiction didn't mean that I was destined to be a failure as a father.

I can still remember the night we brought Tristan home from the hospital. I leaned over the side of his crib, a young new father looking at his very new little boy. It was dark, and Tristan was sleeping soundly, his little butt in the air, arms out over his head, a small patch of auburn hair curling just above his neckline. I felt this incredible weight of responsibility that I think all new fathers feel, but it seemed especially heavy because I thought for sure I was going to blow it.

I even whispered, "Please don't screw this up."

I must have said it louder than I intended, because I woke Tristan up, and it took me an hour to get him back to sleep, and all of that seemed like a sign that I was going to "screw this up" and become a horrible father just like the drug-addicted father I had.

So I suppose you can imagine how shocked I was when Tristan came back home from the park only twenty minutes later—red-faced, agitated, and alone—and announced, "He was saying all sorts of gross stuff and being mean. I told him I didn't like it."

He shoved his black BMX into the bike rack next to our van. He took off his red helmet, his shaggy brown hair a mess. He slapped his mitt down on one of the garage shelves, then folded his arms.

"And?" I said.

He looked up at me and said in a matter-of-fact tone, "He wouldn't stop. So I just went home."

I'm not sure how long I stood there in what could only be described as total shock. I mean, wow! The whole time he just looked me straight in the eyes, shoulders rigid. Everything about his posture said, "I did exactly what you told me to do."

I got dizzy, struck with this simple thought: *You were actually listening to me!* I told him I was proud of him. I even gave him a high five and told him to go into the pantry for some cookies. He became calmer with the mention of cookies.

"How many cookies can I have?" he asked.

"How many do you usually get?" I asked.

"Two," he said.

"Double it," I said. "And a soda!"

I almost winked but decided against it. I didn't want to sour this new taking-my-advice thing with one of my dad moves.

As he went into the house to get four cookies, I stood there in the garage trying to figure out where this kid came from, and I couldn't help but think back to that first night with him as a baby. In the blink of an eye, it was just over a decade later, and I was a 30-something father of three who'd had a pretty rough childhood and was trying to figure out how he raised a little boy that would look a peer in the eye and say, "Stop or I'm leaving."

I couldn't help but feel like this moment was some sort of a turning point, from my wondering if I was screwing up as a dad because I didn't know any better to realizing that I might actually be doing it right. It was a pretty awesome feeling. Awesome enough that I went inside, sat next to Tristan, and had myself four cookies and a soda.

CONFESSIONS OF
A STAY-AT-HOME DAD

In bed we discussed the logistics one more time—when she would leave, when she would be home, and when she would do homework. She reminded me about the kids' library day, Norah's dance class, and swimming lessons.

It was my first summer after finishing graduate school. I now had this big-kid, after-college university job, but it had a nine-month contract, so Mel was going to summer school full-time while working an internship and I was going to be a stay-at-home dad to our four-year-old daughter and six-year-old son.

As Mel spoke, all I could think about was how clean our apartment would be. How I wouldn't put up with the kids' crap. I was 29 and cocky, and I had no doubt that I was going to nail it as a stay-at-home dad, even if it was only for a few months.

We lived in a small, stuffy, third-floor apartment with three bedrooms, no air-conditioning, and a shady 4-foot-wide deck that overlooked the Corner

Mart in a small Oregon town. As we spoke, we could hear our pot-smoking neighbor having sex with his girlfriend next door in oohs and aahs and occasional Italian. Our windows were open and we had box fans running, and the smell of the first floor's charcoal grill wafted into our apartment.

We'd been downsizing.

I'D MADE IT MY GOAL TO WHIP OUR APARTMENT INTO SHAPE DURING THE SUMMER, AND ALL OF IT WAS UNDER THE ASSUMPTION THAT TAKING CARE OF OUR TWO YOUNG CHILDREN FULL-TIME REALLY COULDN'T BE THAT DIFFICULT. RIGHT?

We'd lived in the apartment for almost a year. The plan was to save up to buy a house, but with the kids, and Mel in school, and my being on just a nine-month contract, saving had been taking far longer than we anticipated. The tight space turned even little messes into eyesores. Cereal bowls sat on the table while toys, pajamas, *Spider-Man* underwear, and more toys covered the living room floor. It wasn't dirt as much as it was kid clutter. Mel had been a stay-at-home mom for about three years, and in our old, larger townhome, these messes didn't seem as bad. But with the summer heat and the smaller apartment, they seemed worse than ever.

I'd made it my goal to whip our apartment into

shape during the summer, and all of it was under the assumption that taking care of our two young children full-time really couldn't be that difficult. Right?

I'd finished graduate school. I was close to 30 and hadn't missed a car payment or rent payment or credit card payment—really, any payment on anything—in close to ten years. I wore a tie and slacks to work, along with real leather shoes. Outside of that temporary cramped apartment, I was feeling pretty good about my accomplishments.

Taking care of my own kids when I wasn't working outside of the home should be no sweat.

"Are you even listening to me?" Mel asked. "I'm trying to tell you how to take care of our kids."

"Yeah," I said.

"Really?" she asked. "What did I say?"

"The same stuff you've been telling me for days," I said. Then I went on about how things were going to be a little different while I was at the wheel. I told her how I wasn't going to put up with the kids' crap, and how I had plans to clean and organize the apartment because I'd have so much free time.

"Don't worry. I got this. I'm going to crush it. Like Thor, but with a vacuum. I mean, honestly, how hard could it be? They're my kids."

Mel looked at me and said, "Really? I just hope our children don't die." She paused for a moment. Then she said, "Or kill you."

"You obviously don't have a lot of faith in me," I said.

"No," she said, "it's not that. I just know our children better than you, and they are little psychos."

MEL LOOKED AT ME AND SAID, "REALLY? I JUST HOPE OUR CHILDREN DON'T DIE." SHE PAUSED FOR A MOMENT. THEN SHE SAID, "OR KILL YOU."

She was right. I didn't know our children all that well. Particularly Norah. She was born a few months before I began graduate school, and most of her childhood up to now had been a blur. Until that summer, I'd been finishing two graduate degrees consecutively, working as a graduate assistant, and doing odd jobs at a children's book publisher. I didn't know the names of Norah's friends, which stuffed animals she preferred, or if she liked her toast cut in squares or triangles. Worse yet, I didn't know if she really liked me. I wasn't around enough to call myself a quality father, which was a fact that'd been weighing on me and I hoped to remedy by being a stay-at-home dad.

Mel sat up in bed and said, "You think you're going to do a better job than me, don't you?"

I didn't want to say those exact words, but I did naively assume that taking care of my own children couldn't be that hard. But to be real, Mel obviously didn't have much faith in my abilities to manage our house. I don't think either of us were shining too brightly as husband and wife in this conversation. But you know, it's always during the transitions that things come out sideways for us.

I didn't agree with her, but I also didn't disagree. I just kinda shrugged and twisted my lips, letting the question drift out one of our open windows.

Mel didn't get mad. She didn't laugh at me or tell me I was wrong. All she did was poke me in the chest and say, "They're going to destroy you."

And it was right then, in that moment, that I began having something to prove.

During my first day as a stay-at-home dad, I demon-cleaned. I vacuumed, scrubbed toilets, and washed dishes. I showed Tristan and Norah how to make their beds, clean the living room, and clean the playroom. I expected it of them. I let them eat only healthy things for lunch—peanut butter sandwiches made with whole wheat bread, Mandarin oranges, oatmeal, and baked chicken. My life was a checklist. I cleaned the tub, and once the tub was clean, I knew I wouldn't have to worry about it for some time. I mean, really, how dirty could a tub get? It was soaking in soap most of the time. I felt this way about most of what I was working on. I vacuumed under the kitchen table. Check. I wouldn't have to do that again for what . . . a week? Same with the dishes, the laundry, and the living room. And for the first few days it worked.

The kids listened to me because I was this new, slightly frightening authority figure in their lives.

Mel came home to a tightly run ship, and I looked at her smugly, lip curled. I wanted her to see how wonderful I was doing. I wanted her to know that I was the master of this house, the best stay-at-home dad ever!

AND I DID HOLD MY OWN. HECK YES, I DID . . . UNTIL DAY FOUR, WHEN I STARTED TO REALIZE MY CHILDREN'S HEADS MIGHT AS WELL HAVE BEEN LAWN SPRINKLERS THAT SHOT GARBAGE AND TOYS INSTEAD OF WATER.

And she admitted it too.

"Wow!" she said. "The apartment looks great. Good luck keeping it up."

She gave me this smirk that only furthered my convictions. *"Good luck," indeed!* I thought. *You just watch, little miss. "Good luck." This will be the cleanest summer in history!*

And I did hold my own. Heck yes, I did . . . until day four, when I started to realize my children's heads might as well have been lawn sprinklers that shot garbage and toys instead of water. I cleaned the living room, turned around, and saw that the table was covered in sticky crumbs. I cleaned the table, and suddenly the living room was messy again. I asked Tristan and Norah to keep their toys in their rooms and eat over plates, and the moment I turned my back, all the toys rushed out again, along with food from the pantry. I insisted they use napkins and they insisted on using their sweet napkin pants.

With every rule I tried to enforce, even the simple ones that were needed to keep the apartment clean, they acted like I'd taken away a basic human right that was needed to sustain life, like air or water.

Things came to a head on day six because of Ringo the puppy. We had breakfast, got dressed, and around 9:30 a.m., we started picking up the living room. Tristan put his *Pokémon* cards away, and I asked Norah to pick up her shoes.

"Ruff. Ruff," she said. She was on all fours, panting, her little butt waving like a tail.

"Norah. We don't have time to be a dog. We need to get things cleaned up so we can go to swimming lessons."

"Ruff. Ruff."

She'd done this puppy thing before, and although it was cute when we had time to be a puppy, right then we did not have time to be a puppy. Not that time and place to be a puppy mattered to her. We could've been evacuating the apartment because of a fire, or going underground because of an impending nuclear blast, or running from a gang of bloodthirsty zombies—it didn't matter, in Norah's mind, there was never a bad time to be a puppy.

"Listen to me," I said. "We have forty-five

minutes to do our chores before swimming lessons. Just pick up your shoes. This isn't complicated."

She barked at me again, and suddenly I got really irritated. Didn't she understand that we had a limited amount of time? Didn't she know that after swimming lessons was dance class? This was the only time we had to clean. So much rode on these 45 minutes. One messy day and Mel would assume she'd won. She'd come home, see the toys in the living room, the food on the floor, and the dirty dishes in the sink and conclude that I'd fallen short.

WE COULD'VE BEEN EVACUATING THE APARTMENT BECAUSE OF A FIRE, OR GOING UNDERGROUND BECAUSE OF AN IMPENDING NUCLEAR BLAST, OR RUNNING FROM A GANG OF BLOODTHIRSTY ZOMBIES—IT DIDN'T MATTER, IN NORAH'S MIND, THERE WAS NEVER A BAD TIME TO BE A PUPPY.

Unacceptable.

I asked her again—only this time, with more force.

"Norah. Pick up your shoes. It is not that hard. You're not a dog. You are a little girl with hands. Pick up your shoes, walk on your hind legs, and put them away." I couldn't believe I'd said "hind legs," but it made sense at the time.

"Ringo wants to play fetch."

"Ugh!" I yelled. I clenched my fists at my sides.

"She's just being a dog," Tristan said. "You don't have to get so angry."

Now Tristan was back in the room, sitting on the sofa, watching and not cleaning.

"Dude," I said. "Don't you have work to do?"

He shrugged, and kept watching.

Everything was going off the rails because of Ringo.

I looked down at Norah, who now had her shoe in her mouth, the business end against her tongue, drool dripping down the sole of the shoe.

"Oh, kid!" I exclaimed. "Don't put it in your mouth. That's disgusting."

I tugged at the shoe, and she clenched down with her jaw, holding the shoe and growling. Norah and I fought over the shoe, me pulling on the heel and her clinching down harder, eyes open wide and slightly crazy. I don't know how long we fought.

I finally picked her up, jerked the shoe from her mouth, carried her down the hall, and dropped her on her bed. My tense body, the anger in my face, everything about that moment showed that I was flaming mad. Norah had to have known that I meant business, right?

Nope. Not one little bit. Nothing about this moment fazed her. Instead of saying she was sorry, instead of falling in line, she laughed. High, happy, childlike laughter that showed she was having a great time. Then she asked if I would do it again.

"Do what?" I asked.

"Throw me on the bed," she said. Then she barked and panted, her tongue out, and until that moment I'd never wanted to drop one of my children off at the pound.

I shut Norah in her room and walked away, hopeful to get a second to clear my thoughts. But she opened the door just wide enough to stick her face out and started howling. I tried to block her out and get things cleaned up, assuming she'd eventually stop, but she didn't. She just kept going until our apartment manager knocked on the door and asked if we had a dog, which wasn't allowed.

I told him that it was just my daughter pretending to be a dog, and he gave me this I've-heard-that-story-a-million-times sort of look, and by the time he got done looking around my apartment for a dog, it was time for us to leave.

That evening Mel came home to a messy house, an irritated husband, and two whiny children. She walked through the kitchen, into the living room, her eyebrows raised. "Rough day?" she asked.

"We had a little setback because of Ringo the dog," I said. "But I will get things back in order by tomorrow."

Mel made a clicking sound. "That Ringo has ruined several of my days. Did you put Norah in her room?"

"Yes," I said.

"Did she keep barking?"

"Yes."

I told her about how the apartment manager searched the apartment for a dog, and she nodded and mentioned that he did the same thing to her a couple of weeks ago. "I find things go a lot smoother if you just spend a little time listening to her," she said.

"I didn't have time to listen to her," I said. "We needed to get going."

"Hmmm," she said. "Let me know how that works out for you."

I scowled.

The next day, I decided to take it up a notch. I cleaned the apartment and took the kids hiking.

Our first hiking adventure went great. The kids were excited to do something new. We saw a bald eagle, some ants eating a dead mouse, unidentified animal poop, and a waterfall.

The clean apartment and how I'd managed to get the kids to exercise impressed Mel, and I'll admit, I gloated. I went on about how it was no big deal, and how I had this whole thing under control.

I started taking the kids on a couple of hikes a week, which was great at first. But then they became death marches. Tristan and Norah constantly asked when it would be over and if I could carry them. They dragged their little feet and sagged their shoulders. One of them was always hungry, tired, or thirsty, regardless of available water and snacks. Norah constantly needed to pee while Tristan always needed to poop. Once Norah wet her pants and sat down on the dusty trail, covering her crotch with pee-soaked mud. Then she insisted that I put her on my shoulders because her legs were tired.

I argued for a bit, but eventually I did it. So help me, I put that pee-pee mud monster of a kid on my shoulders. . . .

"Dad, let's just go home, this place is stupid" was more or less Tristan's refrain on each hike.

Once we made it to our destination, whether it was a view of the city or a staircase waterfall, Tristan whined until we turned around, while Norah tugged at my pants to proudly show me her wet crotch.

I needed some peace and quiet and thought just maybe I could get that in the bathroom. But every time I went, Tristan and Norah came storming in, demanding a Popsicle or an argument be settled or to simply stare at what I was doing, confused and amused, as if my business was obviously their business. They pointed, asked questions, made assumptions—but mostly they just laughed. I started locking the door, and that worked for a time. But then they started sticking their little fingers beneath the door.

"Dad! Can you see them?"

Eventually, the kids got wise and anticipated

my restroom visits. I'd go to shut the bathroom door and suddenly a small hand or foot would block it. I'd yell at them to leave. I'd threaten to ground them. But it didn't matter. I had to go and they wanted in for the show.

One night after a hike, as Mel came home from school, Tristan was crying because I'd taken the iPad away, and Norah had peed her pants. The floor was strewn with Cheerios, crackers, clothing, shoes, board games, and DVDs. The tub had a ring. The apartment smelled of rotten milk. I was at the table, head down, massaging my temples.

Mel didn't rub it in. She didn't call me a failure or anything like that. She just rubbed my back. Her eyes seemed to say, "You've hit bottom. I understand. I've been there."

One month into being a stay-at-home dad, and all I did was drink Coke Zero and bitch. My lust for cleaning had dwindled. I started to accept my failure. I ate an alarming amount of ice cream. I allowed the kids to watch what they wanted so I could sleep warmly in my bed, away from what my children were becoming: lazy slobs like myself.

It was on one of these resting days that Norah came in with her toy doctor kit. She placed her soft hand on my face and said, "You need a checkup."

She gave me Bun-Bun to hold. Then she checked my eyes, ears, blood pressure, and temperature. She leaned in close, her face to the side, her eyes peaceful and concerned. And as she worked, I thought about what Mel had said earlier in the summer: "I find things go a lot smoother when you listen to her."

"You need a shot," she said. "But it's just a little one. It won't hurt."

She gave me a shot in the leg with a large blue and yellow plastic syringe. Then she raised her arms and said, "All better. You can get out of bed and play now!"

Funny thing was, I did feel a little better. There was a sweetness in what she was doing that made me feel hopeful.

When Mel came home that night, I put it all on the table.

"I admit it. I'm a horrible father. How do you listen to them?"

She wasn't smug about it. She didn't look me in the face, smile, and say, "How hard could it be?" She didn't tell me that I was pathetic. I suppose she didn't need to. I was telling myself all of those things already. Instead, she sat across from me at the table and said, "You're not a bad father. It's just that our kids can suck sometimes. I mean, I love them. But they can really suck."

"Tell me about it," I said. "Really frustrating."

"I find things go a lot better when I don't worry so much about the house. I just focus on listening to them. Ask them what they want and try to use that to get what you want." She gave me a few examples, like how Norah would clean up the living room more willingly if you whistled at her and pretended that cleaning was a game of fetch. And that Tristan would clean up the living room if you gave him a few extra minutes of video games for not complaining.

She gave me a number of other tips to help with the kids, and as she spoke, all of it sounded familiar. These were the same tips she gave me before we switched roles, only this time I was listening.

We connected that day. I'd spent some time in her shoes, and it did me good. I thanked her for the advice. She smiled and said, "Thanks for listening."

Things went a little more smoothly after that. I tried the whistle method on Norah, and it worked. So what if she was carrying everything with her mouth? I didn't care anymore. I knew it was the best way to get things done. Once, when she threw a fit and I had to put her in her room, I thought about her love for animals. I went and got a cow puppet. I sat on her bed with the puppet on my right hand and in my best cow voice I said, "Norah, my name is Dr. Cow. I have a PhD in tickles and hugs. Why are you so sad?"

Norah unloaded on Dr. Cow. She told him how Tristan had scared her by making a funny face. Then he didn't apologize. "He just made me really scared," she said. Then she gave Dr. Cow a hug, and then all three of us went and chatted with Tristan to resolve the problem.

TRISTAN COULD TELL ME THE DAMAGE ON NEARLY ANY POKÉMON. HE KNEW THE WATER TYPES, AIR TYPES, AND ELECTRIC TYPES. HE KNEW THEIR BACKSTORIES AND THEIR HOMELANDS. AND YET, IF I ASKED HIM ABOUT SCHOOL, HIS DAY, ANYTHING OTHER THAN *POKÉMON*, HE SAID HE COULDN'T REMEMBER.

Dr. Cow started making regular appearances. He made things go much better with Norah.

Tristan was a tougher nut to crack. I didn't know how to get him to want to talk to me. So I asked him about *Pokémon*, the one thing he loved—and I hated.

Tristan could tell me the damage on nearly any Pokémon. He knew the water types, air types, and electric types. He knew their backstories and their homelands. And yet, if I asked him about school, his day, anything other than *Pokémon*, he said he couldn't remember. But what I think bugged me the most was that I didn't feel I could connect with him in any other way than to talk about *Pokémon*. I thought about how wonderful it would be if the two of us could talk about the news or politics or literature. But he was six. So most of the time, he told me about *Pokémon* while I mindlessly nodded.

So I started reading a little about *Pokémon* online. Nothing too in-depth, just enough to feel like I could engage in the conversation. I tried hard to shove my hatred of *Pokémon* deep down inside. And I practiced talking about it without using the words "stupid," "irritating," or "ridiculous." (This was difficult, I assure you.)

One night as we had dinner as a family, Tristan started talking about *Pokémon*, and I listened. I asked him about different creatures and trainers. I told him about some of the regions I'd read about. He raised his eyebrows and smiled. We went back and forth.

Then I asked him about his friends at school and which one would make the better Pokémon trainer, and he told me that Samantha would be the best trainer.

"Why do you say that?" I asked.

"I don't know." He paused and thought for a moment. "I think because she can run really fast. And she isn't very tall, so she could hide behind bushes. And I just think she is smart and has a funny laugh."

The corners of his mouth twisted, and Mel and I looked at each other with raised eyebrows.

I asked if Samantha was his girlfriend.

"No way," he said. "I just think she's funny. And

I like when she smiles. And sometimes she pushes me on the swing."

He paused again. "It'd be really fun to catch Pokémon with her."

He folded his arms, put his head down, his cheeks a little flushed, and I knew the conversation was over.

"Samantha does sound like she'd be a great trainer," I said.

Tristan smiled. Then he picked up his plate, walked around the table, and hopped on my lap. We ate like that for the first time in months.

Across the table, Norah told Mel about her new friend, Dr. Cow, and how he gave really great hugs. Mel smiled, looked at me, and whispered, "Dr. Cow?"

"He has a PhD in tickles and hugs," I replied. "They've had a few appointments."

Mel nodded, half a smile on her face.

Books, movies, and toys lined the table. We'd shoved them to the side to make room for our plates. The sink was full of dirty dishes, the floor was sprinkled in cereal, and the living room looked like the stuffed animals had had a blowout party. I didn't care, because for the first time I felt like I understood my kids.

After Tristan and Norah went to bed, Mel and I sat at the table. We talked about our days, and I told her life was going a lot easier after taking her advice.

"You're doing a pretty good job at this stay-at-home dad thing," she said.

"Thanks," I said. "I'm sorry for not listening the first time."

CRAZY THINGS MY CHILDREN HAVE SAID TO GOD

I have tried so hard to raise my children in a religious home where they understand God enough to fear him. And yet, my children have said some crazy things to God, usually while blessing the meal, and often when we have guests. Most evenings we have dinner together and the kids take turns giving the blessing. We've done this for years, and let me just say, if a rational adult said some of the following crap, they'd have become a leper. But with children? Obviously they can say whatever, and God does nothing while my mother kicks me underneath the table because I'm obviously not raising my kids right.

Here are a few examples (names have been removed to protect the sweet, innocent children).

Please bless that Dad will stop sucking at *Mario Kart*.

Bless Grandma, because sometimes old
people die.

Thank you for *Pokémon*.

Thank you for Roblox.

Have you seen us all naked?

I don't like chili, but bless it anyway.

Thank you for iPads.

Goodnight, room. Goodnight, moon.
Goodnight, cow jumping over the moon.

Please make our dad love the dog.

Make them take us to McDonald's.

Bless everything except the napkins,
because they're stupid.

Alexa! Bless the food!

Can you please just make the yucky food
mac and cheese?

If the food has poison in it, make it not
poison. Make it chocolate.

I'm sorry for making the dog smell my fart.

Please don't let the vultures eat me.

Thank you for DORITOS.

Please make tomorrow my birthday.

Please bless that everyone will hug Mom,
but not Dad, because he makes us use
napkins.

Thank you for Netflix.

Why can't I touch the matches?

Please bless that I can get past world eight
on Mario.

Do you watch us poop?

Make Mom have another baby. Please!
Please. Please . . .

Please make real corn taste more like
candy corn.

Dear heavenly Santa . . .

Thank you for Mommy.

Thank you for Daddy.

Thank you for unicorns.

Amen.

See what I'm talking about? After each prayer, Mel and I mention what they should and shouldn't say to God. The kids nod, and then the next meal comes along, and bam! Sacrilege.

I'm going to hell. . . .

HOW TO GET
THE SEX TALK
VERY, VERY WRONG

Norah and I were discussing the dog's boner. Not that I wanted to discuss it. I don't think I've ever wanted to discuss a dog's boner in the history of my life. Frankly, I'm not into that sort of thing, and I'd like to think that she wasn't either. But she was nine, and curious, and asking a lot of questions about anything and everything; and unfortunately, as discussed previously in this book (see page 44), our dog was a sexual deviant and his around-the-house lovemaking raised a lot of questions.

Norah and I walked into the living room for different reasons. She was looking for her math book, and I was looking for my wallet. But our missions got sidetracked when Norah said, "Dad, Pikachu's doing it again."

I looked at what he was doing, sure. But I didn't need to. I'd heard "Pikachu's doing it again" enough times from enough family members to know exactly what he was up to.

Norah froze, her face twisted, eyes open wide, almost like she'd walked in on a murder. Only it was our dog, murdering our furniture with his . . . you know what, I'm just going to stop this simile right here.

I CAN THINK OF SEVERAL TIMES BEFORE WE STARTED PUTTING HIM IN THE KENNEL AT NIGHT THAT I'D GET UP FOR A DRINK OF WATER ONLY TO WALK IN ON A DOGGY-FURNITURE ORGY.

In our living room was a small black dog kennel with a sleeping mat. This was where Pikachu slept at night. Part of the reason we put him in a kennel to sleep was because he couldn't be trusted not to make love to random objects in the night. He'd basically turned our sofa, easy chair, decorative pillows, random stuffed animals—anything fuzzy and soft—into his love slave. I can think of several times before we started putting him in the kennel at night that I'd get up for a drink of water only to walk in on a doggy-furniture orgy. It felt like the whole house was contaminated with his love, causing all furniture to be suspect and making me feel guilty each time a guest visited. They'd sit down, and I'd wonder if I should tell them—but ultimately I didn't, because it wasn't exactly a conversation starter.

It was a little out of control. I spoke with our vet about it, and she basically said it was a phase. And sadly, I knew that Pikachu's favorite partner wasn't our furniture, or Norah's favorite Build-A-Bear llama, Midnight, or the chew toy shaped like a poop emoji, but his own dog bed. He'd tug it out of the kennel and then have his way, the stuffing shooting out the opposing end with each thrust. Morning, afternoon, evening, the time didn't matter—nor did who was watching. His sexual desires really couldn't be contained. And I suppose it was only a matter of time before Norah started asking questions.

Pikachu paused as we entered the room, still hunched over the dog bed, and looked up at us, his brown eyes guilty and shameful and full of desire, his tail between his legs, fully aroused and breathing heavily.

Then he turned his back to us, almost like he was inviting us to watch, and went back to work.

I told him to knock it off, and he froze once again. I took away the dog bed, and put it back in the kennel, and then let him outside to "walk it off."

I turned around to face Norah. She was in jeans with a unicorn stenciled on the knee and a turquoise matching unicorn print T-shirt. She had braces and bangs, and everything about her said, "I'm nine." But what she asked seemed older than that for some reason: "Is it dangerous?"

She bit her lower lip.

"What?" I asked.

"His red thing?"

I laughed, just slightly enough to be noticeable. It wasn't a "you're foolish" laugh, or a "this is awkward" laugh (although the situation was awkward), it was a "I have no idea how to handle this" laugh. But she didn't interpret it that way.

Not at all.

She assumed I was laughing at her question, which, to a preteen girl, is very easily interpreted as, "I'm laughing at you." She looked up at me with this furrowed brow and went to run upstairs, embarrassed. Suddenly I was left wondering if I'd just ruined everything and she was going to grow up all sexually confused and twisted and in need of years of therapy to get over my laughing at her because she asked if the dog's boner was a threat.

"Stop!" I yelled. "Don't go upstairs."

She paused near the entrance to our stairway.

"I'm sorry. I wasn't laughing at you," I said, my hands up and open, palms out. "I was just laughing about the fact that I didn't think this was how it would happen."

I must have seen a million sitcoms where some bumbling father winds up having the sex talk with one of his daughters. He stumbles through, getting it more right than wrong. And I always laughed at those TV moments, because they seemed so sweet and heartfelt, and I assumed at some point I'd be having this talk with my daughter.

But nothing about what was happening felt sweet or heartfelt. I actually felt awkward, and nervous, and a little fearful. I was sweating. Maybe I assumed it would happen differently. The last thing I ever wanted as a parent was to be sitting next to my daughter talking about how sex works, the nuts and bolts of it all, and trying to make the moment meaningful as our horny, small, brown family dog walked off his boner in the backyard.

But does anything with parenting work out as expected? Not in my experience.

THE LAST THING I EVER WANTED AS A PARENT WAS TO BE SITTING NEXT TO MY DAUGHTER TALKING ABOUT HOW SEX WORKS, THE NUTS AND BOLTS OF IT ALL, AND TRYING TO MAKE THE MOMENT MEANINGFUL AS OUR HORNY, SMALL, BROWN FAMILY DOG WALKED OFF HIS BONER IN THE BACKYARD.

Maybe if I were better at scheduling things, this would've all gone smoother. Perhaps if I'd actually sat down and decided to have the talk, did some reading in preparation. Perhaps if I'd found some informative videos and got a whiteboard. A PowerPoint, maybe. Perhaps then I could have made it more educational, meaningful, and ultimately had more control over the situation. But like most parents, I dreaded moments like this.

I wasn't exactly sure how to bring it up or how to end it. The middle seemed a little murky too. So when sex did come up, it was usually unannounced, and I had to shoot from the hip and hope I didn't mentally scar my children. With Tristan, it came up after he hit me in the balls at the grocery store. He was also about nine years old. We were shopping, I made a stupid joke. He tried to shove me, but accidently hit me in the crotch, and I buckled over, and I couldn't breathe for a moment.

I WASN'T EXACTLY SURE HOW TO BRING IT UP OR HOW TO END IT. THE MIDDLE SEEMED A LITTLE MURKY TOO.

Anyway, I got mad at him, and he started asking questions about why it hurt when he did that, which led to us discussing boy parts and girl parts, and how his boy parts would change. All of it circled around what the boy parts do, and how they connect with girl parts, and by the time we made it home from the store I was using my fingers as a diagram in our driveway, both of us red-faced. Our elderly neighbor happened to be watering her lawn as I sat in the driveway, my index finger cupped in my hand, sliding it in and out, my son looking at me with the same horrified, blank face Norah gave Pikachu as he humped his dog bed. As I awkwardly waved at our gray-haired neighbor, Tristan ran out of the van and into the house, and she gave me this confused look that assured me the days of her dropping off homemade bread were over.

Tristan and I had a few more conversations about sex after that, which went much better, but the whole situation in the van scared both of us.

But poor Norah. She started asking questions around the dog's boner as if it were a threat, and I just didn't see how this sex talk wasn't going to result in an epic fail.

"How what would happen?" she asked.

"The sex talk," I said.

She looked at me with straight-up terror, almost like she also knew someday we'd have this talk, and she was obviously dreading it as much as I was. It seemed like something I should have had Mel involved with, but she was working at the school garden with Tristan and Aspen, so it was just the two of us, alone, discussing the inevitable.

BUT POOR NORAH. SHE STARTED ASKING QUESTIONS AROUND THE DOG'S BONER AS IF IT WERE A THREAT, AND I JUST DIDN'T SEE HOW THIS SEX TALK WASN'T GOING TO RESULT IN AN EPIC FAIL.

I sat Norah down at the table. I got her a peanut butter cup, because it just felt like she should have some candy to make this easier.

"No," I said. "The dog's boner isn't dangerous. Although, I must admit, his dog bed might disagree."

I laughed at my own joke to ease the tension, but it didn't work.

"Do all boys have those . . ." She paused for a moment, searching for the right word but having difficulty. "Things?"

I threw out a few proper words for it, but eventually said, "Yes."

She shivered as she opened her peanut butter cup. Then she paused for a moment, and asked, "All of them?"

"As far as I know," I said.

"Why?" she said.

I shrugged. "Because they do."

She asked if men were the same size and color, and I did my best to explain that the shades and sizes vary, although I wasn't an expert. She wanted to know what it was for, and why it happens. I did my best to discuss the intricacies of the birds and the bees as our dog scratched at the patio door. I was surprised by how much she already knew about sex. Some of it she'd heard from friends, or from TV shows, or from YouTube vloggers. She mentioned reading a kids' book about bodies that answered some questions. It seemed like she'd put together this puzzle of what sex was. As we talked, both of us seemed to be getting more comfortable. We were speaking freely, and those awkward feelings were almost gone. I was feeling pretty good about our relationship, because she obviously felt safe discussing this sort of stuff with me. Until Norah interrupted me midsentence to say, "Ummmm, Dad . . . he's doing it again."

I turned to my right, and sure enough, Pikachu had wandered back into the house because I hadn't shut the sliding door. He'd pulled out his dog bed again, and he was doing his thing, right there, with both of us at the table. And once again, I dragged him away from it, put the dog bed back, and sent him outside to walk it off—only this time I shut the door.

I sat back down at the table, put my hands in my face, and asked, "Where were we?"

She didn't respond for a moment. I peeked through my fingers, and saw that she also had her face in her hands, and for whatever reason it felt like we were connecting somehow.

Then she asked something that I didn't expect. "Are all boys like that?"

"Like what," I asked.

She pointed at Pikachu. He was standing next to the patio window, on the lawn, staring at us with this fixed, creeper-like concentration, an erection between his legs, brown eyes crazy with lust, still breathing heavily. And suddenly I thought back to her earlier question about if the dog's boner was dangerous, and it felt like what she was really asking was, "Are men dangerous?"

I thought for a moment, and I will admit, it was difficult to think with the dog looking in on us like that. Then I said, "Some guys are just like Pikachu. But not all of them."

I told her how some men are just in it for sex, and they will do it with anything, even the sofa. I told her that they will say sweet things, sometimes all the right things, to get sex. I told her sex is important, and it is a significant part of a rewarding relationship. "But it isn't the relationship," I said. "There's so much about you that is valuable. I need you to know that. What I want for you is to find someone who's interested in partnership. Someone who is interested in all of you, mind, body, and soul. Not just sex."

She thought as I spoke, processing my advice. Then she looked at me and said, "So what you are saying is, 'Don't look for a Pikachu.'"

I laughed. "Yeah," I said. "Exactly."

MORE LIES
I'VE TOLD
MY CHILDREN

Sure, I lied a lot around Christmastime (see page 49, for example). But, you know, lying doesn't have to have a season, right? You can lie to your children any time of the year, for really any reason—as long as they are harmless white lies that make your life a little easier, prevent fits, and make your children believe you have superhuman powers.

Are those enough qualifiers?

If not, I have some examples that might help.

You wouldn't like my Skittles. These ones are really spicy.

The batteries in this toy are unique. We can't buy more of them because they only make one set, so we're going to have to throw this noisy thing away.

Yeah, I know you really wanted to go to Disneyland this summer, but it's closed for cleaning, so we are going to visit Grandma.

If you don't play outside every day, your legs will fall off.

No way! The tooth fairy didn't forget about you. She only works odd days of the week. That's why you didn't get a dollar last night.

No! No! That's not an ice cream truck. It's a music truck. It sells music.

It's actually illegal to eat Cap'n Crunch® until you are 21. I know it sucks, but I don't want you to get arrested.

Pulp Fiction is a documentary about oranges. You wouldn't like it.

It's impossible for you to get your head through the long sleeve of your pajama top. (This really isn't a lie, per se. I was just proven very, very wrong.)

Nope, that cat isn't dead. Cats just like to sleep on the side of the road sometimes.

Oh gosh, please stop crying. Look . . . voilà!
I flip your toast over, and the butter is gone!

The McDonald's ice cream machine is broken.
(This is a lie only 20 percent of the time.)

The door at the grocery store opens
automatically because I'm a Jedi. (My kids
believed this for a year, and it was the best
year of my life.)

That picture you drew is the best picture
I've ever seen in my whole entire life!

Oh wow! That's too bad. Only people who
are allergic to ice cream get a headache
while eating it.

I downloaded an app the other day that
will tell me if you really brushed your teeth.

Me: Your twin brother refused to clean his
room too.
Kid: I don't have a twin brother.
Me: Not anymore. . . .

Yeah, MAYBE we can go to Chuck E.
Cheese . . . tomorrow.

The thing is that there's a power shortage,

so we are going to need to go to bed early to save power. That's why they call it daylight saving time.

Oh no! That wasn't me. The dog must be gassy.

If you roll the window down on the freeway, you will be sucked out of the van.

If someone really loves you, they will eat one of your chicken nuggets to make sure they aren't poisoned. I may have just saved your life. You're welcome.

See? Totally harmless. Unless they are in their 30s and still think Skittles are spicy. But hey, that might be for the best. I wish I thought Skittles were spicy. I'd probably have a sexy bod instead of a regular dad bod. The real concern here is that eventually your children get too smart for this sort of thing, so my suggestion is to take full advantage of it while they are young.

LISTEN, SON . . .
WE SERVE PEOPLE
WE LOVE

When I asked Tristan to help unload dirt from our small pickup into his mother's new garden boxes, his reaction was typical.

"Ummmm, I'm busy right now," he said.

I'd told him that I was expecting his help earlier in the day, so he knew this was coming. But on-brand, he acted like that conversation never happened and was playing Roblox on the family laptop, lounging on the sofa with his feet on the coffee table and wearing the "outfit": blue hoodie with black and white track pants with a hole in one knee.

In so many ways, I didn't really want his help. Not that I didn't love my son. If you've made it this far in the book, I hope you can tell that I love him and I want him to grow up to be the best Tristan he can be. But at the same time, getting him to become someone who can leave my house and function on his own has been one of my biggest challenges, and there are so many times that I know, in the core of my everything, that if I'd just do something myself, it would take half as long and be half as stressful.

But with this garden box thing, I needed his help. We'd moved into a new house a few months earlier, going from one side of our small Oregon town to the other. At our old house, I'd built some garden beds for Mel. But it was too difficult to move them to the new house, and the new owners wanted them anyway, so I decided to just build new ones. Which, across the closing table, sounded like no big deal. But when I built those garden beds at our old house, I was in my early 30s. I was now in my late 30s, just shy of 40, and I underestimated how much my body had decomposed in that time.

A week before I asked Tristan to help haul dirt, I was at the park with Aspen, watching some young twenty-something father play tag with all the kids. He was jumping off the equipment and going down the slides. He was really into it.

He kept giving me this squinty look that seemed to say, "Why aren't you out here? Why aren't you more engaged?"

In my head, I was like, *Listen, twenty-something dad. You're awesome. I give you props. When I was a young dad, I did all that. But now my back hurts, and I get shin splints pretty easily, and my hemorrhoids grow agitated with even the gentlest of physical activity, and that's without chasing my kids on the playground.*

What I'm getting at here is that my body was sore before I built the garden beds. Then it became even sorer after building the garden beds. My legs were burning from hauling the beds from the garage to the backyard, and the thought of unloading the dozen or so truckloads of dirt alone would be a slow death.

I needed Tristan's help.

I MADE THREATS THAT WERE LAYERED IN THREATS. I OFFERED HIM A REWARD ONCE THE WORK WAS DONE. HE TOLD ME MAYBE AFTER HE FINISHED THIS LEVEL. HE EMPHASIZED THE "MAYBE."

So I sat next to him on the sofa in my work pants and gloves and asked him again. This time he ignored me. I told him that I needed his help. I told him that it was a lot of work, and I couldn't do it myself. I told him that my back hurt and my hips hurt and my arms hurt, and he would be doing me a huge favor by helping out. I told him that he was expected to do this as part of the family. I told him that I would take away his screens for the rest of his life.

I made threats that were layered in threats.

I offered him a reward once the work was done.

He told me maybe after he finished this level. He emphasized the "maybe."

He was testing his boundaries, which is something all children do the moment they leave the womb, so you'd think I'd be used to it by now. But I don't know if parents ever get used to it. Much like how my body was wearing out, fighting with my son was starting to wear my patience thin.

Around this time, I was in a group chat with some other parenting bloggers. One member of the chat was a recently single mother. She mentioned that her preteen daughter pulled a similar move awhile back by refusing to put down her phone and do the dishes. My friend was so stressed out adjusting to her new life as a single mother that she ripped the phone out of her daughter's hand and smashed it with a hammer. I couldn't help but look at my son ignoring me and want to do the exact same thing with our family computer.

I took a breath. Then I took my son's hands off the keyboard, shut the computer, and took it from him. He reached for it. He fought with me. He got mad, and complained, and said he was in the middle of a game.

But eventually, he followed me outside to unload the truck.

Moments later, we were next to a wheelbarrow, shoveling dirt into a flower bed. We hadn't talked for almost 30 minutes, and if we accidentally made eye contact, he looked at the ground.

I wondered if I'd taken it too far. Not that I hadn't turned off his games before—surely I'd done that. My real concern was that he now felt resentment toward me, and all of that was going to translate into him resenting doing work for other people. Or work at all. I worried about this sort of thing a lot actually, and I often wondered if it was going to result in Tristan becoming this lifeless slug of a middle-aged man, still wearing the same track pants and hoodie and never getting off my couch.

He looked at me with expressionless eyes, his hood up, his shoulders slumped, and said, "Why do we have to do this?"

I leaned against my shovel and thought for a moment, because I'll admit, it was a valid question. Neither of us were all that into flowers or vegetables or any of the things that would grow in those garden boxes.

Mel was the gardener.

I thought, and he waited, and finally I said, "When you love someone, you serve them."

I went on, telling him that I want him to grow up to be the kind of man who serves the people he loves.

"This," I said while gesturing to the dirt, and the garden boxes I'd built earlier, and the wheelbarrow and shovel, and the first of many truckloads of dirt we would unload over the next few weeks, "is what love looks like."

He didn't like my answer. I could see it in the

way he reluctantly picked his shovel back up. We unloaded two more truckloads of dirt that Saturday. He rode with me to pick them up, and we worked side by side for several hours, but he hardly spoke. And in that silence, all I could feel was his resentment.

Nevertheless, Tristan helped me finish unloading the dirt. And when we were done, I thanked him. I told him I loved him, and he gave me a reluctant side hug. On the whole, though, I assumed this moment of teaching my son why he should serve other people was a huge fail.

The next day, while I was at work and the kids and Mel were enjoying the day off because it was between terms, Mel sent me a picture that was taken through the back window of our living room. It showed Tristan in his blue hoodie, his shaggy brown hair a mess, unloading a wheelbarrow full of dirt into one of the garden boxes all by himself.

Mel told me that she'd picked up another load of dirt, and before she had a chance to unload it, Tristan voluntarily started working. When she asked him why, he shrugged and said, "Because I love you."

I'd never been prouder of my son.

ACKNOWLEDGMENTS

A huge thank-you to Marissa Giambelluca, my editor. You continue to believe in me, for some strange reason, and I am confident that you will one day speak with a therapist about it. Your time, encouragement, and careful constructive comments have meant the world to me, and I do honestly think the world of you.

Thank you to the good people at Page Street for caring about my work, and giving me an outlet to send it into the world. You were the first publisher to take a risk on me, and you continue to do so. I love you for it.

Samantha Angoletta, and all the good people over at Scary Mommy, I owe you so very much for your continued support of my work, and your continued willingness to publish my contributions. Honestly, and truly, thank you.

Mel, you are my muse. You are my everything. You are the most supportive and wonderful person I have ever known and will ever know. Thank you for sharing your life with me, and thank you for allowing me to write so candidly about the life we share.

Lastly, but not least, Tristan, Norah, and Aspen. You are my goober kids. I love you. Every time you ask, "Are you going to write about this?" and I don't answer, I need you to realize that the answer is "Yes." You are the most interesting people I have ever met, and as stressful as this whole parenting gig has been, you three are the best part of it. Thank you for allowing me to share our lives, and thank you for helping me to grow into a father.

ABOUT
THE AUTHOR

Clint Edwards is the creator of the daddy blog No Idea What I'm Doing, and author of the books *I'm Sorry . . . Love, Your Husband* and *Silence is a Scary Sound*. He is a staff writer for Scary Mommy and a parenting contributor to the *New York Times*, the *Washington Post*, and *Parents* magazine. He has been featured on *Good Morning America*, the *TODAY* show, *The Talk*, and *The View*. Kelly Clarkson finds him hilarious, a fact he brings up regularly when having dinner with extended family. He lives in Oregon with his wife and three children.